"The week after _____ Chuck _____, school, I won the Colonial Open — my first major win in over two years. He showed me that I have all the answers right here in myself."

Peter Jacobsen
PGA Tour Professional

"S.E.A. is a program to help you bring out the potential that you have in you."

Mary Beth Zimmerman
LPGA Tour Professional

"S.E.A. has helped me change my thinking on the golf course from 'this game is going to drive me crazy — it's impossible, unfair' to 'a game of creative fun and challenge.' I'm having fun again."

Johnny Miller
PGA Tour Professional

"S.E.A. has put the fun back into my golf game. I feel much more creative and positive on the course than ever before."

Mike Reid
PGA Tour Professional

"S.E.A. is having a major impact in sports, why not be a part of it?"

D. A. Weibring
PGA Tour Professional

"I went into the S.E.A. school with high expectations and came out with those expectations drastically exceeded."

Kenneth Blanchard
Co-author of *"One Minute Manager"*

You don't have to join a cooperative model of performance and draw upon the resources of unlimited minds.

You can remain in a competitive model. You can do it all by yourself.

How much time do you have?

5 DAYS

to

Golfing Excellence

by Charles Hogan
with Dale Van Dalsem and Susan Davis

T & C Publishing
Sedona, Arizona

ISBN:0-9624504-0-5
Library of Congress catalog card number: 85-090499

Editor: Merl K. Miller
Cover: Hal Wood
Illustrations: Greg Ellingson

T & C Publishing
P.O. Box 2788
Sedona, Arizona 86336
1-800-345-4245

Formerly published by
Merl K. Miller & Associates
ISBN: 0-933557-07-8

Contents

To my father and mother for not telling me about things that I could not accomplish.

Foreword

As the founder of International Management Group, I have worked with countless athletes. I have seen the best, the worst, and everything in between come and go. An attitude of self assurance and trust in their abilities is evident in those athletes who get to the top. By the same token the first thing that happens when performance starts to fail is the deterioration of that attitude.

Several years ago, I picked Peter Jacobsen to become one of the most productive personalities in all of sports. In May of 1984, after winning the Colonial Invitational, Peter excitedly told me that a group called Sports Enhancement Associates had shown him how to tap his inner resources. I was further impressed when Peter went on to win the Greater Hartford Open and have, by far, his best year ever.

Peter isn't the only person I know that benefited from S.E.A. training. For instance, D. A. Weibring and Raymond Floyd have had similar experiences. D. A. has had his best year ever and Ray has knocked at the winner's door nearly every week since he completed S.E.A. training. The course, designed for both professionals and amateurs, is not limited to golf. For instance, Betsy Nagelsen credits S.E.A. with her win of the World Mixed Doubles Championship in 1984 and the Women's Doubles Championship in 1985. S.E.A. teaches athletes to find supreme confidence in whatever game they play.

Five Days to Golfing Excellence helps you gain this same confidence and actually helps you learn how to play golf. It offers you the same training that has benefited many professional athletes. I firmly believe that Chuck Hogan's insights and training in the use of mental skills to play and perform your best are a major advance in athletic achievement. I encourage you to participate at the forefront of performance excellence, whether you aspire to athletic fame or the maximum enjoyment of pure recreation. Don't just read this book — use it! This is what they don't teach you at any golf school!

Mark H. McCormack
Author of What They Don't Teach You
At Harvard Business School
September 1985

Introduction

The most outstanding feature of my career as a professional golf instructor is the recognition that all golfers have the same obstacles and frustrations to enjoyment and performance. Professional players like Peter Jacobsen and Mary Beth Zimmerman are distinguished from amateurs as much by vocational choice as by natural ability. Most importantly, the frustrations of all these golfers are artificially imposed and can be disposed of much more easily than has ever been suggested before. My primary goal in founding Sports Enhancement Associates was to help golfers and other athletes realize their true potential.

Five Days To Golfing Excellence is about playing golf. I do not stop at the golf swing. In fact, *golf swing* is only one simple concept in a series of learning steps that leads to true enjoyment of the **GAME**. There are five days of learning and relearning that will help you foster and enjoy the creative process in every shot and every round of golf thereafter.

Critical to this process is a new way of processing information about the shot and the shotmaker. You will introduce all your senses into the creation of golf shots. The recognition and management of these sensory images will replace old and destructive verbal dialogue. Imagery is the true language of your brain and body. Your ability to observe this process will make you a true player of the game. You'll become both the teacher and the student, and you'll learn to put mechanics in their place. You see, the entire golf instruction society says "Keep your head down", as if the problem were somewhere outside your head. The physical mechanics of golf are widely taught. Grip, posture, alignment, swing plane are all standards of beginning golf instruction. In this book you will learn how to combine mental mechanic skills with your understanding and execution of physical skills to enrich your enjoyment and grasp of your golf game.

The basic concepts introduced in this book have a sound neurological basis. I asked one of my students, Chris Moran, to give me a scientific explanation of what happens in S.E.A. training. Dr. Moran practices medicine in St. Louis. In addition, he is an Associate Professor of Clinical Radiology at the Mallinckrodt Institute of Radiology. He has had an interest in brain functions and neurology for a long time. He has written several papers on the topic and is on the staff of Deaconess Hospital in St. Louis as a neuroradiologist. Here is what he said about S.E.A. training:

　　S.E.A. begins with a basic explanation of the golf swing but goes far beyond in the search for golfing excellence. This program introduces a new system of thinking for the golfer (which also has applications to many other situations in life). Having become committed to this approach, you will be able to devote your full attention to control doubt, fear, *nerves,* and other golfing horrors. All golfers have the wish to play to their level of ability.

　　Science has shown that humans have the capability of controlling physiological processes by controlling their brain wave patterns. Utilizing the sounds on the tapes, you will synchronize your brain waves enabling you to relax so that the resultant stress free environment will allow your mind to pay full attention to the creation of images. These fully orchestrated images will involve all of your senses to create positive situations which allow you to experience your full potential. When playing, success will have been experienced as you have already *been there.* The testimony of the touring professionals asserts that the S.E.A. program works for them. Faithful application of these principles will enable you to play to your full capability.

If you would like to get a similar benefit from S.E.A. training, then you should study this book as well as read it. It is intended as a five day self-study course on golf. I urge you to set aside five consecutive days when you can spend at least one hour a day reading and studying a single chapter of the book. On Day One, I'll show you how to relax and feel good about your game. You'll learn to make golf a sequential learning process and you'll learn how to enjoy yourself on the course. Although the main thrust of this book is the mental side of golf, I still feel that swing mechanics are important. However, you need to see your golf swing in the proper context. I'll show you how to do this on Day Two. On the third day, you'll learn what an image is and how you can benefit by using images. You'll start to apply these techniques on the fourth day. Be sure to do *all* of the exercises on Day Four. You'll pull everything together on the last day and you'll learn to keep things in perspective.

As you go through this course I'll show you how to create images, and I'll give you some relaxation techniques. I feel that most of the material in this book can be self-taught. I know that you will gain immediate benefit starting with the first day. However, if you want to get the full benefit of the course, you should listen to the tapes produced by the MS III image generator. The sounds that you will be listening to on the cassettes produce a *frequency following* response in your brain wave activity. Your brain waves will harmonize into the slow-wave predominance known as alpha and theta waves of 4 to 12 cycles per second. Within this potential you will access a magical insight that gives you the supreme confidence of seeing the task completed before it is. This is followed by the inevitable compliance of physical accomplishment.

Each chapter of this book is illustrated with both cartoons and stick figures. I have used stick figures for a number of important reasons. First, golf swing is easy to learn. There are only a few things a golf club is designed to do. You need to focus your attention on the golf club, not on the person holding the club.

Second, when you pay attention to an infinite number of body positions, you deny the possibility of conceptualizing the function of a golf club. You will continually search for answers where they do not exist. Your body is a symptom of the problem, not the cause.

Finally, it is impossible for you to liberate the enormous capability of your subtle mind when you are intellectually involved with how you should swing. You cannot consider the target if your attention is on yourself. The important elements are the club, ball, and target. After the fundamentals, that is all there is to it. The stick figures de–emphasize you and let the important learning surface.

Relaxation

Before you do each exercise in the book, go through a General Relaxation Exercise. The *Mindshapes* relaxation and imaging tape has a relaxation program on the A side. It includes the narrative of the following exercise. If you are not using *Mindshapes* it is a good idea to either record the exercise or have someone read it to you the first few times until you are familiar with the process. At first this will seem very mechanical but you will get the hang of it shortly. You will notice yourself getting more relaxed, and you will also notice as you go from day to day that you gradually increase your lungs' capacity to take in more air. Once you feel you have achieved a relaxed frame of mind you can turn your attention to the actual exercises. You will notice then that your breathing changes naturally to a pace and depth of its own.

General Relaxation Exercise

Lie down or sit in a comfortable position.

Close your eyes.

Turn your thoughts to your breath. Breathe deeply. Take air in through your nose and exhale through your mouth. Let your stomach move out freely, and completely fill your lungs with air.

Synchronize your breathing with your heartbeats. Try this now. Breathe in slowly through your nose for six heartbeats.

Inhale the air deeply into the bottom of your lungs. Hold your breath for three beats. Keep your shoulders and neck relaxed.

Exhale through your mouth for six beats.

Wait for three more heart beats and begin the cycle again.

And relax . . . . In six . . . hold three . . . out six . . . hold three . . . .

Imagine that you are inhaling a vibrancy that cleanses your lungs. It permeates your lung walls and filters throughout your body. Let this vibrancy swirl through areas that are painful or tense. Expel all discomfort as you exhale.

Let your body relax deeply . . . , deeper than ever before.

Take note of images that appear: what colors you do see, what textures do you feel, what temperature changes do you notice, what do you taste?

Relax even more and let the tension out . . . .

Do you feel lighter or heavier?

Let your mind wander. Continue breathing deeply and freely.

Relax and feel the vibrancy travel through your body.

Now it is in your muscles, now in your bones, now in your blood stream.

You can do anything. You can be anywhere.

There is no need to make things happen. They happen naturally.

Relax. Know that your images are always there.

Listen, notice and enjoy. Continue to breathe freely and relax.

Sequential Learning

This book also gives you a learning or relearning sequence that leads to a concept of how the golf club **must** be swung. Up to this time, you have probably learned a multitude of rights and wrongs. Just as you get one part right, a different part breaks down. However, the only thing that really matters is the design of the club. In fact, *the design of the golf club is the only master model of the golf swing.* When you let the design of the club design your swing concept, your body will fall into symptomatic compliance. Your mind will be free of any extraneous thoughts, your body will be in a relaxed posture, and you will receive all the appropriate information from the target and its conditions. Now the fun begins. You react to the target. You are it and it is you. This is where great golf has and always will be played.

Chuck Hogan
September 1985

Day 1

After The Swing, There Shall Be Golf

"S.E.A. training was the most enlightening experience I've had in golf."

Raymond Floyd
1984 S.E.A. Graduate

What the world needs is a new golf creed. It might read something like this: **After The Swing, There Shall Be Golf.** To be played well, golf must be played creatively, and this sign, mounted on the signpost of every number one tee would remind all golfers to play the game, not the mechanics.

Creativity is not limited to *creative people.* Webster says "to create" is "to produce or bring about by a course of action . . . to produce through imaginative skill." When you create, you project form and function into a blank or formless space. Painters, inventors, sculptors, musicians, computer programmers, electrical engineers, mountain climbers, and golfers are all creative; they all use skill to produce a result. The professional golfer is a Mozart, a Picasso, or a Hemingway. Players like Peter Jacobsen, D.A. Weibring, Johnny Miller, and Barbara Mizrahie have the ability to create a shot in their minds and execute it precisely with their bodies. Winners like Mark Lye, Mike Reid, Carolyn Hill, Mary Beth Zimmerman, and John Cook have a genius for conceiving, creating, and executing an appropriate shot.

To Create Is to React

You create when you gather information about a theme or situation, reflect on it, and then react to it. Your reaction is triggered by inspiration that has been fostered by your past experiences and perceptions. You react and create when you sing in the shower, return a tennis serve, build a bookshelf, cook a gourmet meal, and stroke a golf ball into a hole. You may think this doesn't apply to you because you're not creative. But you are! It is only the vocabulary and the curriculum you presently use that keeps you from being a creative golfer. You have kept yourself from being a creative golfer by thinking that you *act* toward the golfing target instead of *reacting* to it.

You would probably agree that a Larry Bird last–second, off–balanced, double–teamed, leaping, turn–around, twenty–foot swishing jump–shot is a reaction to the target in its purest form. His body gyrations are not something he thought about, but a part of his reaction. He is so intensely in tune with his target, so engrossed in his communication with the basket, that his body does whatever is necessary to make the shot. A winning golfer does the same thing with his target but so subtly that it is not recognized as a reaction because the vocabulary of golf is mechanically oriented. The language of golf has led you to believe that the reaction isn't important.

Try to imagine golfers and their instructors chopping up the actions of a driver as he negotiates a car around a curve. Driving would no longer be as simple as responding to the input of the road and its conditions. The dialogue coming from the booth might sound something like this: "Yes, folks, this is a great day for driving. The pavement is a nice black surface without being too hot. He's lining up his turn now. Notice that there is more pressure in the left hand. The left elbow is folding nicely into his lap as he pulls down on the steering wheel. Notice the right hand releasing and being positioned under the wheel. There is an excellent hinge of the right ankle as his foot rises off the accelerator. What a beautiful execution of a mild left-hand turn. The car is still in its own lane." Obviously, you got beyond this when you first learned to drive, but have you gotten beyond this point in your golf game?

Golf Swing or Golf Game?

In your daily life, you constantly perform very complicated actions and maneuvers which are reactions to being an open receiver to information. This is routine activity and a simple matter of reaction. It is only from the viewpoint of an outside observer, and the descriptive dialogue, that the activity takes on fragmentation and complications. As with driving, dissection of a golf game can make it seem overwhelmingly complicated.

You would have to have a distaste for life to be the passenger in a car whose driver attempts to operate his car in the same mechanically oriented way he operates his golf clubs. Instead of responding to the road, he is talking his way down it with the deliberation of his intellect. If there are any unknowns presented or pressures introduced, he'll intellectualize the car into the ditch, the highway's equivalent of a sand trap!

The same is true of any activity that requires precise calculations for performance. You respond efficiently only when you remain receptive to information being provided by the target or the task at hand. If you shift your attention to yourself, you take attention off the target. This shift cuts you off from the very information you need for precise reaction. Focusing entirely on the components of any self action — walking, throwing or eating — will disrupt and destroy your efficiency. Ben Hogan's putting woes resulted from just such intellectualized focusing and the ensuing self–awareness.

Golf instruction has become an institution of self-awareness rather than target-awareness! Golf lessons, golf publications, golf commentators, and your golfing partners continually tell you what is wrong with some piece of your swing. You are continually bombarded with the notion that somehow you will be more accurate in relation to the target by thinking of your arm, head, leg, or club position.

This whole institution is not a conspiracy. Most people sincerely want to help you play well. It's just that we are all a product of our education. Dissecting the whole to see how each part works is a hallowed part of education. Science couldn't do without it, and the eighth grade wouldn't be the same without cutting up frogs in biology class. The problem arises only when you keep on dissecting for the sake of dissecting.

Some years ago an observer watched the beautiful shots of a great player of yesteryear. He observed the physical components of the swing precisely because he was not privy to the internal workings of the mind responsible for the reaction creating the shots. His act of observation began the dissection of the golf swing, and it has continued and been deified ever since.

In golf instruction, you need to learn to put the parts back together. You need to be taught golf, instead of golf swing. There are some dramatic differences between golf swing and golf:

> Golf swing is focused on self
> Golf is focused on ball to target.
>
> Golf swing is and is being taught as an act.
> Golf is and ought to be taught as a reaction.

Go React! Go Create!

If you agree that reaction is more efficient than fragmented actions, how do you get there without sacrificing the golden calf of golf swing mechanics? All professional athletes learn the fundamentals, but they don't stop there. The key is not to draw a veil between yourself and the target. You can identify and improve upon a component of action, but this process must be short–term, stored and put back into the whole action.

In fact, golf presents a wonderful opportunity to become a receptor of information. You have a wealth of time to process information at your own rate, according to your personal pace. When you play at a creative level, you take information and respond to it. You calculate factors of distance, ball lie, elevation, and wind, and then select your club. As you position the ball, your mind synthesizes the information for your response. As you align and waggle the club, you *see* or feel the shape of the shot and let the strike of the shot happen as the *picture* or feel provokes your swing and guides your motion. You must surrender to this intuitive process.

You don't need to talk to yourself to do this. In fact, self–talk indicates that your attention has shifted back to self and away from the target as the guidance system. It is a warning that you are acting, not reacting. Simply let the *feel* of the target bring forth your reaction; be reactive to the target, conditions, and yourself. Don't separate yourself! Keep these things in mind:

> Self–talk separates.
> Self–awareness must be in a non–target environment.
> The golf course is a target environment.
> You are a part of the target!

One week after just such S.E.A. training, Peter Jacobsen won the 1984 Colonial by being a careful listener, or receptor, to the greens. The 15th green said "Chip, Chip," but Peter's intellect decided to putt during Saturday's round. That putt did not go in the hole. On Sunday, the 15th once again said "Chip, Chip." This time he listened and chipped the ball in the hole.

Listening and reacting require practice, perhaps more than the mechanical method. At first you will feel that you have made a shift from physical mechanics to mental mechanics. Reassure yourself that reaction or *blending* with the target is the approach, and it is how the best golfers play the game. You will need considerable conviction to resist the appeals of the golfing institution to re–enlist in swing mechanics. Assign it to the appropriate practice green, back yard, and living room, its appropriate environment, and reserve the golf course for creativity.

On the golf course, no two shots are exactly the same. You must be pliable and reactive to the conditions of the target. The perfect golf swing on the golf course is the one most adaptable to the subtleties of each shot. The perfectly repeated swing observers are so fond of only functions effectively on the practice tee where everything is always the same.

On the golf course, you must be reactive. As you approach the course for the day's play, be receptive to the environment. Drop the traditional ideas of beating the course, scoring, and beating opponents.

Warm up your total being on the practice tee. As your muscles stretch and warm, feel your deep breathing enrich your blood and relax your body. Engage your mind in the conditions of the day. Take note of the temperature, wind, humidity, and textures.

On the putting green, hit some 20 to 40 foot putts. Let the distance, slope and speed of the green *line you up*. Soak up information like a child listening to a bedtime story. Let the details of the story become brighter and brighter. Strike the putt in relation to the information you have quietly received. Review the putts by judging only the quality of the information you received, not by judging the characteristics of your physical stroke. Let the modification of succeeding strokes be based only on your reception of information. Let your stroke react.

Approach the first tee with the same attitude. Let each shot be a new story. Take in the pieces and react as the details of the story climax, compelling your motion. Review and judge your performance as a receptor, not as a doer. Go about playing the game and be your own judge. There is no support system for your new approach. Your own productivity and new–found enjoyment of the game are your own lasting rewards. You are, after all is said and done, out there to *play* the game.

Is Golf Mental or Physical?

Golf is both mental and physical. Your body only does what your brain commands. What you observe your body doing is the outward observable production of your brain's actions. Your body is not independent.

Your eyes do not see!
Your ears do not hear!
Your mouth does not taste!
Your fingers do not feel!
Your nose does not smell!

Your brain deciphers all of the information provided by your eyes, ears, mouth, fingers, and nose. Your sensory organs are merely receptors for brain information. If you were to unscrew your hands and lay them on the table in front of you, would they be able to feel? Without your brain, your body wouldn't be able to feel, taste, act, or react; your body demonstrates and expresses the work of your brain.

What you call physical is thus both mental and physical. Our language by cutting up this process makes you believe that there are two systems instead of one. The name *ear*, for example, is a description of a physical feature not a function; *hear* is a description of mental function, but *listening* is, in reality, both mental and physical. It cannot occur without the cooperation of mind and body.

Your Biocomputer

Here is another way to look at it: consider that you are a biocomputer. Your brain is the computer hardware, your body is the print–out, and your images are the software. Your body will do what the software programs it to do. That's assuming that all the parts are oiled, greased, and plugged in. Since your body performs in accordance with the images it receives from your brain, you owe it to yourself to take as much interest in the quality of your images as you do in the food that you eat. All facets of you, the biocomputer, are responsible and *on* when you engage in a round of golf. You must take the same care with the software you program into your golf game that you take when you choose food for your meals or fuel for your car.

Because you are a biocomputer, all action is preceded by an image just as all action in a computer is preceded by the activation of computer software. But there is no time–lapse between the thought and image which activates your neuro–transmitters and the ensuing physical movement stimulated by the image. Images in your brain occur simultaneously with physical responses, and because these images happen at the same time as your physical action, it is easy to forget what your brain did, with the result that you focus on your body doing something. A perception like this is incredibly limiting to your ability to create good golf. Remember *all action is preceded by an image.* You must understand this underlying truth before you can manage your game. If you really believe that you are not responsible for either the function of your mind or the function of your arm, you're always going to have problems with your game.

Make Golf a Sequential Learning Process

Let's put mechanics in a reasonable sequence of learning, as we would if we were going through school. In nearly all skills there is a relatively short period of intellectual learning accompanied or followed by a short–term conceptual understanding or development. The purpose of the intellectual and conceptual periods is to liberate the creative activities of the learner. You can tap the enormous potential of your skills only in the creative element. It is this element for which the game was invented. This sequential learning process could be outlined like this:

The Sequence For Learning

	GOLF	WRITING	DRIVING
Analytical & intellectual	Grip/Posture/ Routine approach to the ball	Formation of: letters, words sentences	Location of: steering wheel, pedals, etc.
	(Graduate)	**(Graduate)**	**(Graduate)**
Conceptual	Function of club design	Components into composition	Press gas for fast, brake for slow, turn wheel for direction
	(Graduate)	**(Graduate)**	**(Graduate)**
Creative	Create the proper shot for a given condition of the target at hand (Win the Colonial)	Create a letter, article or book (Win a Pulitzer Prize)	Drive as needed for the conditions (Win the Indy 500)

Complete a grade and graduate, then complete another grade and graduate, and so on. In this way you can move from primary subjects into creative realms. But if you never graduate, you'll be stuck in a primary activity. If you never graduate from the primary skills of grip, posture, and routine, you never move to the creative skill of playing the game; you'll never be a reactive golfer.

Golf is a game, not just the physical skills used to play it. It should be learned in a total sequence like any other skill. Consider how you learned to write reports. You learned to type in TYPING 101, 8th grade in Ms. Compton's room on the third floor of your beloved Junior High. With text in tow, you tackled the second row "Type **f** with your *left first finger* and **j** with your *right first finger.* Hold your curved fingers lightly above the home keys. Type **f** with a light, quick stroke and release the key at once. Next, type **j** in the same way." Great! Now you know how to type. But when Mr. Jones assigned the report on Custer's Last Stand, your skills at the typewriter took a backseat to your ability to read about the topic, be impressed by the information, form opinions of the climate of the time and the gravity of Custer's situation, decide whether you sided with him or the Sioux, develop an approach to your report, write it, and, finally, type it. Your emphasis in writing your report centered on the report itself, not on your typing skills. The physical skill of typing was only one very small part of the creative activity of report writing. The physical skill of golf swing is only one part of the creative activity of a golf game. Your golf game is the creative part of your involvement in golf. Practice on physical mechanics is akin to learning the second row of keys on a typewriter. Chipping a shot out of tall grass, over a bunker, with the flag three yards from the edge of the bunker is, well, actually, your last stand. You write the book with every shot you make on the golf course. First you write it, then you type it. First, the story and then the club selection, grip, posture, and stroke that puts it onto paper and onto your score card.

Be a sequential learner:
Intellectual
Conceptual
Creative

The learning sequence has been in place for eons in every skill except golf. Typing involves the intellectual analysis of placing your fingers on the keys and making the proper movements of your fingers. With this intellectual learning comes the conceptual understanding that you type so you can put written material on a page. These two learning processes are fundamentally necessary if you are going to move to the creative level and sustain proficiency.

The creative level of any activity is the object, the very reason to be involved with the game. Discovering and liberating your abilities in the form of good shots and low scores is the essence of motivation. It is like the exhilaration of graduation day from school. Finally, you can look towards creative application of all the intellectual and conceptual knowledge you developed inside the academic environment.

Unfortunately, traditional golf instruction does not consider concept. Therefore, you may be stuck in the intellectual phase as the only avenue to remedy a problem. Occasional glimpses of creative golf (fun and proficient) have no support from the conceptual process, so it falls apart.

The appropriate sequence is:

Pre–swing mechanics
Golfswing concept
Creative shotmaking

Whether you are a pro or an amateur, when the score is important, management of your mind/body language of imagery is the key to success and the only answer.

To learn a skill, you need to take one step at a time. It's most efficient to stay with each step until it's thoroughly yours: inside–out, backwards and forwards, in your sleep and learned. Before we delve into mental mechanics, let's consider an overview of physical mechanics. Let's discuss the typewriter before we discuss story–writing.

Five Things to Know
About Golf Mechanics

Learning or relearning, the following rules apply:

1. Don't do any mechanical function unless you understand why it works and why you are doing it.
2. Practice at least 60 repetitions per day for 21 days.
3. Give full attention and intention to each repetition.

The Master Model of Your Golf Swing

The first key concept relates to how the club hits the ball. Take a few minutes right now and repeat the two elements of this concept over and over again. Force them into every level of your mind:

1. **Only the club hits the ball — you don't!**
2. **The ball reacts only to the club — not to you!**

Once you understand these two simple precepts, the mechanics are very simple. If you do not understand these two concepts, then you will become a victim of the endless options of what *you* should do, and you will become hopelessly lost and frustrated.

The second key concept about golf mechanics consists of three parts.

The ball goes wherever it goes as a result of:
1. **ClubFACE direction at impact**
2. **ClubPATH direction at impact**
3. **Clubhead VELOCITY at impact**

This is exactly the same in tennis, ping pong, raquetball or *any* other game that uses a flat surface against a round ball.

The third concept is a little more involved:

1. **If you are mechanically proper before you swing, you will probably make a proper swing.**
2. **If you are mechanically improper before you swing, you will probably make an improper swing.**

The reason is simple and logical when you think about it. Your entire swing takes about 1.5 seconds. If you are right before you start, there isn't enough time to go wrong. If you are wrong before you start, there isn't enough time to get it right. All of this is magnified by the much shorter duration of the forward swing — the only place it counts.

The fourth concept is a little longer, but also simple and logical:

> **What your feet, elbows, hips, arms, knees, and other body parts do during the swing are the *EFFECT*** of your conceptual understanding of club design and function *NOT* the *CAUSE*.

Just as the relationship of nouns and verbs is the result of the design of the sentence, the swing is the result of the design/function of the club. You understand the design/function of the club, and the swing *goes with*. Learn the intended function of a golf club. Understand how a golf club is designed to work and disregard the human involvement. *The golf club itself is the only master–model of the golf swing.* If you thoroughly grasp and understand the concept of the club's design, you will no more violate that concept than the concept of driving your car. **Your understanding makes the proper swing. The proper swing does not create understanding.**

The fifth concept deals with learning. Golf needs to follow the same progression as any other learned activity:

> 1. **Start with an /intellectual understanding**. Learn the components and pieces. For instance, learn the letters of the alphabet.
>
> 2. **Then graduate and go on to a *conceptual understanding***. Figure out how the pieces go together to form the whole. For instance, how words, paragraphs and punctuation form a composition.
>
> 3. **Then graduate and go on to *creative expression.*** Learn to use your imagination and manifest your potential. For instance, write poetry or short stories.

Creativity cannot be supported without the base of intellectual and conceptual understanding, but neither can creativity be expressed within the intellectual/conceptual realm. Remember:

Golf swing is intellectual/conceptual.
Golf is a creative process.

By understanding and reacting to the club design you will be able to swing. Your swing will reflect your understanding. Your left arm will be straight and your right elbow will fold. You will have balance, rhythm and a beautiful follow through. But you won't care because you'll be so involved with the creative level to which you have now graduated.

Mental Mechanics For Your Best Play

Look at mental mechanics as the tools to open up your creativity with golf. These tools are readily accessible to anyone willing to set aside regular time to practice and develop them. If you are like most golfers, you are quite willing to go to the driving range several times a week, weather permitting or even, in some cases, weather not permitting. But how often would you be willing to repeat Mrs. Compton's typing class? Take a risk: devote more time to mental mechanics practice even if it means that you spend less time at the range. The most efficient practice is 70 percent mental and 30 percent physical. I guarantee you will enjoy golf more and improve your score, if that interests you; or I'll buy you a 1962 Smith Corona typewriter.

Briefly, your mental mechanics practice will involve active research into and development of what's going on *all of the time* in your head: your thoughts. Thoughts are images. You always have images and thoughts. Sometimes they are frenetic, sometimes fragmented, sometimes serene. Sometimes you daydream, create fantasies, solve problems, add numbers, hear the ball go in the cup — all of these mental activities are images. They can be thoughts about yourself, work, golf, sex, your mother–in–law or the pot roast. Sometimes they instill feelings of confidence; sometimes they make you feel as small as a dried–out cherry pit. Sometimes your thoughts are brilliantly clear and sometimes frustratingly foggy and vague. Mental mechanics practice is a technique that you can engage in on a regular, daily basis to heighten your skills at monitoring and shaping your thoughts or images, so that they are advantageous and appropriate from minute to minute and, more to the point; from shot to shot. As you learn to shape your thoughts, your confidence will improve and your game will improve. And that's what you want.

Confidence

What comes first — confidence or good play? — good play or confidence? Confidence comes first. Think about that. And what is confidence?

It's an image or a thought.

It's a feeling.

It's knowing that you have prepared yourself to the best of your ability.

You're swinging well.

Your grip has just the right feel.

You're feeling relaxed, calm, and aggressive.

You've played the course — you have a game plan.

Your dog loves you.

And all is well with the world.

Even Arnold Palmer would have his work cut out for him today.

It's positive self talk.

It's believing.

It's a feeling — of comfort, ease, *rightness*.

It's focused.

It's a flash of intuition.

It's feeling physically flexible — in good physical condition.

It's a lot of other things. Take a few minutes now to think about it and take this space to add your own components of confidence:

What happens when you feel confident? For one thing, you seem to have your rhythm. You have good pacing, and club selection is a breeze. The ball seems to take good bounces. All of your luck is good luck. The putter works. *It's all working today.* You have confidence!

Then it happens. You remark to yourself how great things are going . Suddenly, confidence is lost and elusive for the rest of the round. It's a great disappointment to watch Arnold accept that check at the end of the round. "That should have been mine . . . I really had it in me today. If only I'd . . . ."

Even Arnold Palmer won the 45th PGA Seniors Championship shooting a second round 63 on Friday and then a Saturday round of 79, an incredible 16–shot spread over two days! While you may be consoled by Palmer's difficulties, it is also a reminder that confidence is a frail matter for even the greatest athletes. The very recognition that you may be playing extremely well is likely to destroy the state of mind that you need to continue playing well. Palmer's 79 is not unlike the double–bogey, triple–bogey finish of the average golfer who has realized that if he guards his actions on the last two holes he will have his best score of the year.

Is confidence this fragile? Is it just luck? It can be, but you can change all that. Mental mechanics practice creates image management and makes confidence a more controlled state. Ultimately, you become your own luckmaker.

You're saying to yourself , "Yah, sure — I'm King Kong and I can do anything. I think this stuff is going a bit too far. I mean, I don't have *that* much control. When I play well, I have confidence and when I play bad, I don't have confidence — naturally. It's as simple as that. Forget this mumbo–jumbo that confidence precedes good play."

But the only reason you feel you don't have that much control is because you have never learned to *take* control. It's just that simple. Practice mental mechanics, engage yourself in your images, and build confidence. In this way, you eliminate the prospect of being a victim of your swing mechanics. Start with the confidence that you are mentally prepared and let your body follow suit. Or, if you are still thinking about typing class; attach yourself to the story, not the typewriter.

Degrees of Confidence

Confidence occurs at many levels of intensity and can be recognized during different situations or conditions in any round of golf. Every golfer has a favorite club in which confidence is very high and another club in which confidence is lacking. A certain hole on the course may be a *goat*. You may perform confidently against one opponent with a lower handicap and yet lose to another who *has your number* and beats you often because you lack the confidence in your ability to win. Confidence wanes and waxes differently; the ebb and flow is simply reduced for the frequent golfer.

The two conditions of performance in which confidence is generally not acknowledged are at the polar ends of scoring. When you play a horrible round of golf totally uncharacteristic of your ability, your confidence level is usually not considered a factor. The recognition of confidence as a factor in golf is so non–existent that other symptoms are usually identified and blamed. Poor swing rhythm, extreme discomfort in set–up or swinging over–the–top are typically pinpointed as the *cause* of the difficulties when the real problem is lack of confidence.

Likewise, such descriptions as *out of my mind, perfect timing*, or *I can see the line* may be used to describe a rare and near perfect round. The state of supreme confidence may be overlooked because it is so supreme and powerful, so different from your normal ranges of confidence.

Indeed, most athletes of all sports, and especially golf, would agree that *seeing* and *feeling* the accomplishment of the goal before acting is the essence of confidence and the key to success. You recognize these experiences when you say the putt was *already in* before the stroke was made because *I could see the line* or *I just knew I was going to make it!* On these days when performance is optimum, the fairway is a *mile wide* and greens *huge* and trouble areas are *smaller than the ball*.

Make Confidence Manifest Itself

The job is to make these days of supreme confidence occur more often, to raise the usual range of your confidence. Confidence can't manifest itself if you say things like "I can't feel the club" or "I can't get set." The preconception of success is not there to be followed; it isn't even available. On those days when the putts won't drop, it is evident that the line is obscure and that your body's reaction is equally obscure when you work the putter.

Listen to Kent Myers:

> Its really sort.of threatening to ourselves when we begin to understand that if we're not playing well, we're not thinking well . . . . Accepting that statement calls for a great deal of personal responsibility. It's much easier to say, "Well, I have this or that mechanical problem which I could cure if I could get enough practice." That statement reduces the problem to an impersonal one which makes it not quite so much our fault.
>
> Yet we're forced to take full responsibility for our minds. It's a great deal more risky to say, "I'm not thinking well, or I don't have control of my emotions." We don't have to be quite so responsible if we're concerned only with some little quirk about the way our elbows point. (1)

And on to Jack Nicklaus:

> On the course, I never hit a shot without first seeing the shot completed. I imagine very clearly the trajectory of flight, the reaction of the ball upon landing and the exact spot that it ends up. (2)

Does this mean that your performance levels can be elevated when you attune yourself to the development of your thought and mental imagery processes? **YES!** "The ordinary athlete realizes less than half of his or her potential unless the powers of the mind are utilized." (3) If you are a typical golfer you only focus a small percentage of your mental capacity. "Studies of peak performers demonstrate that their supreme talent is imagery and mental rehearsal." (4) You achieve what you conceive. A new look at the ideas of seeing and feeling will put a whole new perspective on the subject of confidence.

Peak golfing performance requires clarity of, and access to, mental images. **The image *is*** confidence. Performance flows from a state of complete and total immersion in the act of doing. There is no need or reason to be imprisoned by the performance. There is no judgment, for the judge is busy as the witness. This is a state of complete trust where the activities of thought are integrated, merging into harmonic image–making processes. This confident state of mind can be learned in golf as it is in the martial arts — as a function of discipline and flexibility. And as with any discipline, optimal results are simply a matter of commitment and persistence.

Can You Feel It?

Mental imagery is becoming increasingly important in athletics. In the 1984 Olympics, most coaches put a strong emphasis on mental imagery. The East German luge team was a notable example. You may have seen them on television — before they made their run they seemed to be in a trance — their eyes shifted as if they were already actually negotiating their way down the course at incredible speeds. They mentally rehearsed their run exactly, turn for turn, just before they began. This activity was obvious to anyone watching them. You didn't have to be told that it had a dramatic impact on their success; the evidence was right in front of you. The athletes who competed in the biathlon had the task of mentally imaging a calm heartbeat after strenuous physical exercise. They skied cross–country for several miles and then shot at small targets with rifles. Imaging helped them develop control over their bodily processes and instantly slow down a racing heartbeat.

What exactly is imagery? Here's one definition:

Imagery is the internal, non–verbal processing of sensory perceptions which may or may not be externally stimulated. This processing includes all sensory modalities: visual, kinesthetic, auditory, olfactory and taste.

More simply, imagery is thought. Every thought is an image, a picture, a photographic image . If you flick on the light switch in the den, you form an image of that process before you actually flick the switch. You may not be aware that the image precedes the action because it happens so fast, but it does. You drive to the dry cleaners, and you need to make a left turn off Lockwood onto Big Bend Avenue. Before you begin to slow your speed and turn the wheel, you have already formed an image, of yourself making the turn. Your body understands and responds to that image and you pick up your suits before 5:00 without having an automobile accident.

And image is not limited to visuals. When you read the words APPLE PIE, what happens? Does your mouth water? Do you taste warm or cold pie? Is there a scoop of vanilla ice cream on top? Is your stomach rumbling? Have you put the book down and headed for the kitchen yet? Obviously, your thought's pictures are not limited to visuals. They include color, texture, movement, touch, taste, hearing, and smell. Think: *high school locker room*. Can you smell it? Think: *frying bacon*. Can you smell it? Think: *sunburn*. Can you feel it? Think: *windows in your bedroom*. Can you see them? All these are thoughts which can create vivid images for you to which your body readily responds. Read through the following exercise and then go through it mentally. It is meant to involve all of your senses. See what happens for you.

Peeling an orange

This exercise is meant to involve and intensify all of your sensory modes. If you can get someone else to read it to you while you close your eyes and think about peeling an orange, please do so. Begin with the general relaxation exercise from the introduction.

1. See the orange. See its size, shape, color, texture, placement, and environment.
2. Now pick it up. Roll it in your hands, feel the size, weight, shape, and texture. Dig your fingers in and begin . . .
3. Peel the orange. Feel the pulp under your fingernails, the resistance of the skin as you peel it from the fruit. Feel and hear the soundof squirting juice. Let some of the juice run down your arm.
4. Peel the orange entirely. Smell it. Bring it close to your nose and make the odor more intense.

5. Break it into halves, then quarters, and finally into sections.
6. Visually and kinesthetically examine a section. Bring it to your nose, then bite the section in half. Taste it. Feel the juice on your tongue, in your mouth and in your throat.
7. Put the remaining orange back where you got it. Take a napkin and dry your hands and lips. Examine this experience as long as you wish before you reopen your eyes.

How did that make you feel? Did you like your orange? If you have an orange available, now would be a good time to try this imagery *on the course*. Did you use all of your senses?

You Can Create Your Own Images

Mental imagery is continuous and ongoing; without it, your body would malfunction. It forms the basis of your perception,your speech, and your actions. Your images are your perception and your perception is your reality. Your practice of mental mechanics helps you develop an active, conscious role in developing and maintaining images. Mental mechanics fosters imaging and maintains perceptions that generate confidence. Think: *150 yards with a soft draw.* Can you feel the swing that will produce that shot? Mental imagery practice will naturally make the feel of that swing more and more vivid, and your body will have a clear map to take with it the next time you go to the course.

Your Image Rheostat

Even though mental mechanics is new to golf, the language of imaging has existed alongside that of physical mechanics and golf. Expressions like *bite, take a seat,* or *get legs* originated as verbal descriptions of a player's image of what he wanted his ball to do at a particular moment. They provoke images of a ball having teeth and biting into the green, or a ball coming to a quick halt as it sits in a chair, or a ball being carried along on two legs. Originally, *on the screws* or *I nailed it* weren't just mundane verbalizations, but were, in fact, strong, fully developed pictures and feelings of the ball being mashed by the screws of the wood's insert or the picture, sound, and feel of the clubface hammering a nailhead connected to the ball. For the players holding these images in their minds, there was a bodily reaction matching the intensity and vividness of the image. For the originator of the image, there is great meaning in these statements. But, for the rest of us, copying the image, there is little or no particular meaning beyond the comedy. There is no mental/physical engagement which is actually going to help us with the end result of the shot.

The message your mind sends through your nervous system to your physical system is not unlike electricity being delivered to light bulbs through a light switch. For the original imager of *nailing it* the rheostat was open all the way. There was a full charge of electricity moving through the wires and the light bulb glowed at full intensity. But if you imitate another person's image, you are not fully engaged. Although *nail it* may sound charming, it is not your image, so the rheostat does not allow a full charge of electrons. The light bulb is dim. If you play with cliché–type and/or worn out images, your mental commitment to the image is dull. The dull image lacks the required power to send a full charge of neurons to your muscles for the explicit activity you need for a precise shot.

Such commonly accepted images, unfortunately, get more than their share of attention. You may have an attachment to cliché images that work to your disadvantage. *Banana–ball, fat, worm–burner, choke, gagged it,* and *yanked* are more than just words. Even at a low–level image state, there is a corresponding physical response. You cannot say the word *choke* without your mind forming a picture which activates body reactions of restricted breathing, constricted blood supply, tense muscles, and hormonal changes.

It is easy for you as a golfer to say, "Golf is a tough game. Just look at my scores." But as long as you believe that statement, your body has no choice but to react in accordance with the image of your belief, an image that is to your disadvantage. The trick is to find images that are to your advantage, images with the ability to turn the rheostat fully on and stimulate bodily action. This is the cutting edge between pro and amateur, winner and runner–up. Coming to this realization is the starting point of changing your thoughts and game.

What Is an Image?

When you get to chapter three of this book, you'll have an opportunity to examine images closely. But before you finish today, there are a couple of things you need to think about. First, images can be kinesthetic (feel), auditory (hearing), olfactory (smell), and taste, as well as visual. Imaging requires the use of all of your senses, whereas visualization is associated only with sight. Second, images precede internal or external dialogue and are far superior directors of motor skills than self talk. The verbal description of an experience falls miserably short of the actual image or experience itself. The impact of a verbal description of an orange being peeled is far less than the impact of actually imaging yourself peeling one.

If you want to play like a pro, you must do exactly that. If you want to play like a winner, you must be a winner. You must hold the image of swinging like a pro, and more importantly, you must think like a pro or a winner. This means that your images must be vivid, engaging, and individual. You need to practice, on and off the course, fresh and inspiring images which are totally your own. These images can be seen, felt, heard, smelled, and tasted. Don't limit yourself!

To begin with, you can review the clichés used in the game, put real meaning to them, and reform these verbal impressions into a stimulating image as it applies to a particular shot. What do the following *really* mean to you?

Career shot
Hit the flag
A 40–foot snake
Big thunder
Fly ball, fly
Bullet
Pure
Go in!

What picture does each of these convey after you give it deep thought? Does it also have an associated sound, feel, taste, and/or smell? If it does, then adding these other senses will aid in your calculations and in your actual shot–making process.

You may find that the line to the hole becomes a path, a ditch, or a luminescent tube or Mike Reid's path through a row of green worms. Because of your involvement in this well–defined line, the roll of the ball into the hole will be perfect. Allow the flow of intuitive and spontaneous images to enter into your game by triggering your swing plane and motion as well.

You will ebb in and out of your image development. One day the feel of the forward swing will match exactly the brilliance of the image you choose to direct your body. Perhaps the next day it will be difficult to find a strong and vivid image for the shot at hand. Take these days of difficulty as a sign that you need more practice, and practice regularly.

In your daily activity, the thought of playing golf can start a rehearsal of task–accomplishing images to be used on the course. You might consider driving the ball, for example, and take into account the various flight patterns to the target. The ball could *fly* high or *laser beam* low or *float* safely *banking* left to right or *turning* right to left. Throw up 100–foot–high stone walls or a giant hand to keep the ball in the fairway boundaries. Imagine the trajectory of the flight in terms of a cannon's aim, an arrow's flight, or the high lob shot of a tennis ball.

A pitch shot might come down like a paratrooper, a deflated innertube or a dart. Perhaps the shot calls for the ball to take off like a race car or run like a rabbit. Whatever the shot, the image of the shot will need a beginning (the strike), a middle (the flight), and a destination (the hole or target). The image should be as exciting, detailed, and complete as possible.

You can draw from the environment on and off the course. Notice the movement of all kinds of things you see every day. Birds, trains, cars, and bees. Think of the appropriate golf shot corresponding to movement. Sounds, smells, tastes, even the feel of the environment can be incorporated into your shots. Go beyond the mere association of these images into the pure experience of your images. Attach totally to them and experience the ball behaving in compliance with your images. Your enjoyment and efficiency will increase while your effort decreases.

Set aside a few minutes a day for imaging practice. Take one–half hour a day during your personal creative time. Sit comfortably or lie down. Play or practice your golf game in your mind. Hit shots with a variety of images. Keep the images fresh and interesting. Some images will be concrete and others may be abstract in both character and result. You may wish to listen to music while doing this, or you may prefer silence. The more you practice the easier, more spontaneous, orchestrated, and engaging the images will become, and the more pragmatic their use will be as you carry them onto the course. Practice, as always, is the key to success.

Some of these notions may seem a bit bizarre or nonsensical. It could be argued that seeing a ball become a peach, headed right into a peach basket, is not appropriate on the golf course. On the other hand, isn't *The ball soared like a peach headed straight for the peach basket* much more to your advantage than images like *I got slaughtered by Sue after missing so many knee–knockers, that every time I got in the vomit–zone, I gagged like the choke that I am*. These are, after all, just images.

Footnotes

1. Leeson, Del, "Play Better Without Practice," *Golf Digest*, December 1972.

2. Murphy, Michael, *The Psychic Side of Sports*, 1979, Addison-Wesley.

3. Korn, Errol R. and Johnson, Karen, *Visualization: The Uses of Imagery in the Health Professions*, 1983, Dow Jones–Irwin.

4. Ibid.

Success by Design

"How we look at things affects what we look at in very subtle ways."
from *Space, Time and Beyond*
by Bob Toben and Fred Alan Wolf

Success is an image, an image you form of yourself and your accomplishments. Sixteen one–putts is an unquestioned success. A successful self–image projects a successful person to the observer. For the purpose of mental mechanics, success is the ability to have fun, to notice that you get what you think (image), and to enjoy the act of filling in the details. For the purpose of physical mechanics, success is believing that you have a solid foundation intellectually, conceptually, and physically from grip to swing plane so that you are free to play golf, not swing mechanics.

Success is a habit, and success is fostered by habits. I have found a very effective style of forming habits. The formula demands 60 repetitions per day for 21 *consecutive* days. That means 21 days in a row, not 17, miss a day, and then four more days. If you have a break, you won't build a really solid habit that you can hang your hat on. Each of those repetitions needs to be done with 100 percent attention and intention. *Attention* means that you give 100 percent of your mind to each repetition. *Intention* means that you have an understanding and purpose for each repetition. The chart in Figure 1 is designed to help bring this point home. If the chart doesn't bring the point home, your next retreat to the driving range after a frustrating round of golf will. "Here I am again. I just can't seem to get my grip to feel comfortable. I think I'll try shifting my right hand over the top. I've hit the ball — it's duck hooked into Joe Merrill's windshield. I guess I came over the top . . . " You're frustrated because you started out to work on your grip and ended up analyzing your pass at the ball. By fragmenting your focus, you've set yourself up for even more frustration.

A more effective approach is the 21–day plan. The key is to keep it simple and stay consistent. Practice one skill at a time and — **this is very important!** — evaluate only the skill you are working on. If you're working on your grip, it is inconsistent and inappropriate to even care where the ball goes. During each day's practice session you will have images: feelings, specific sensations, pictures, a general attitude. Write these down on a copy of the habit formation chart or in a journal or in a notebook you carry in your golf bag. Keeping a record of your images will improve your management of mental mechanics. Your ability to set a simple plan and stick with it will enable you to enjoy the benefits of the confidence that grows from paying attention to your images centered around one specific topic.

Formula for Habit Formation/Modification in Learning or Relearning Golf

First Basic Premise:	The goal of golf is to get the ball from point (A) to point (B) in the fewest number of strokes.
Second Basic Premise:	Mechanical and attitudinal habits can be formed over the course of 21 *consecutive* days, with a minimum of 60 repetitions per day.
Third Basic Premise:	Active discipline in the 21–day plan will result in consistently getting the ball from point A to point B in the fewest possible strokes provided that:

1) **all** components of physical mechanics (grip, posture, alignment, etc.),

2) **all** components of swing and ball spin concepts (inside–out, club face at impact, the lie angle of the club, etc.) and

3) **all** components of mental mechanics (relaxation, imaging, perceptual flexibility, etc.) are practiced, learned, and habituated in this fashion. (These three items are quite simple to learn and give you a great opportunity to have fun.)

Fourth Basic Premise: After the golf swing, there is golf. This is what makes the habit formation/modification worth doing.

Word of Caution: **Don't confuse the issue. Keep it simple and just do it. That's how it gets done. Do it and then you'll have a habit you can trust.**

Word of Encouragement: **Do this! Graduate and begin to play creative golf.**

Photocopy the chart in Figure 1 and use it to enter specific objectives as you choose them. Start to work on your own objectives. Check off each day as you complete your practice, and remember to start over if you miss a day. Assign the learning or relearning of preswing functions to 21–day allotments. If you are consistent and diligent for 20 to 30 minutes of 21 consecutive days, you will achieve mastery of one component during each 21–day practice session. Grip, stance/posture, and alignment can be finished and assigned to habit. Later, you can assign four to six days each year to evaluate and validate the accuracy of each component, but you won't have to go back to the first grade and stay there —

Figure 1
HABIT FORMATION/MODIFICATION CHART

OBJECTIVE	Beginning Date																				
	1	2	3	4	5	6	7	8	9	10	11	12	13	14	15	16	17	18	19	20	21
Sensitive hands																					

you won't have to go back to the habit forming practice session.

Your next task is to trust yourself. Twenty–one days, 60 repetitions per day, will secure a habit for you. Habits are not fragile. Attitudes are. Habits are hardening of the attitudes. The reason that so many golfers go back to mechanics is because they believe that their swing habits break down overnight. That is simply not the case. When a pro wins a tournament one week and misses the cut the next, do you honestly think it's because his swing mechanics broke down? A better probability is that a link in his attitude broke down. You may be inclined to doubt your swing habits. If so, remember that doubt itself is an image. It is software that you can choose to reprogram and replace with something that is more to your advantage.

It is amazing how golf vocabulary has built a completely inaccurate belief system about your swing. Even the best pros sometimes rush to the practice tee after a poor round, thinking that their swing went haywire between the third and sixteenth hole. When in reality, they can't change their fundamental swing. What really happened is they added tension — a function of attitude. What they actually work out on the practice tee is a shift in attitude.

Form Habits That Improve
Your Mechanics

If you are going to learn to be a creative golfer, you need to habituate grip, stance–posture, and the routine approach to the ball. By turning the intellectual/analytical side of golf into a habit, you'll be able to free your creative side.

The Grip

Grip is an unfortunate word golfers use to describe the act of connecting hands and golf club. *Your hands should connect in the proper position so that they function as the clubface. Your hands and clubface will rotate as demanded by your mind.* Your hands must be sensitive receptors of information. There should be no pressure or lack of pressure. They are just sensors.

I recommend an overlapping grip for most men with average or larger than average sized hands or greater than average strength.

Figure 2

A ten–fingered grip is best for the average sized women's hands, men's small hands, and children or for any person whose hands lack strength.

Figure 3

The size of the golf club grip can and should be enlarged or reduced in diameter to fit your hands perfectly, increasing sensitivity to the clubface and response efficiency to mind command. Very large grips will often *feel good* but actually decrease performance. I suggest that you resist the massive grips unless you have arthritis or nerve damage in your hands. Your club professional can help you determine the proper grip size to fit your hand size.

Mechanically, the correct positioning of your hands is well known. Pick up any golf book and you'll find the basic positions. The fundamentals are:

1. Choke down about one–half inch from the butt of the club.
2. Make sure your left hand is diagonal to the club.
3. Your right hand maintains your finger joints.
4. Your right hand lies down on your left thumb.
5. Vs point at your right ear and shoulder.

Figure 4

What is really important is that your *hands are the clubface.* That's half of the direction of the ball. The formula is clubface + clubpath = direction of the ball.

Always put your hands on the club before you put the clubhead on the ground! Align the leading edge at 12 o'clock while you hold the club chest high. The clubface should be perpendicular to your shoulder lines at all times.

Your hand surfaces must parallel the flat surface of the clubface. Your left palm faces your right palm, and the back

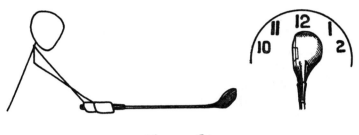

Figure 5

of your left hand is parallel to the back of your right hand. All four of these surfaces are parallel to each other.

When you hold the club like this, you can see that your hand surface is parallel to the clubface surface. Now let's try a little experiment. Hold the club chest high and roll your hands very subtly and then radically. What happens? The clubface's movement parallels your hand movement exactly.

This is a very important concept. If you haven't picked up a club and tried this yet, please do so now. Play with it until you can really feel and appreciate the idea that the clubface always moves in exact compliance with your hands. Imagine at the same time, any of these flat surfaces against a round ball. The ball's direction is dependent upon face/hand direction. The clubface can be pointing in only *one* of *three* basic directions when it contacts the ball: straight, right, or left.

Figure 6

Don't be confused by the shaft between your hands and the clubface. The hand/face relationship is a constant. Imagine that the shaft is nonexistent. The face is at the end of your grip. Any hand movement is instant face movement.

Here is an exercise for you to do to increase your awareness of the hand/face relationship. Read through it and repeat it often over the next few months. It is vital that you increase the sensitivity of your hands to the clubface. Be sure to go through the relaxation exercise before you start this exercise.

Practice Your Grip
(Sensitive Hands)

1. Place your hands in perfect position on the grip of the club.
2. Hold the club up in the air in the position where there is the least strain to your arms and hands.
3. Let relaxation flow through your body into each hand.
4. Feel the alliance and harmony of your hands and the club. Roll your hands/clubface slowly. See/feel how your hands and the clubface are in total and perfect alignment. Whatever your hands do, the clubface also does.
5. Imagine that your hands are warming and that blood and oxygen are circulating and creating more sensitivity in your hands.
6. Sense your hands and the grip melting together until there is no distinction as to where your hands stop and the grip begins.
7. Imagine that a flow of blood and oxygen is actually passing from hand to hand through the grip.
8. Notice that the club and your thoughts are in harmony and in complete compliance with one another.

As you learn or relearn your hand positioning and function over a 21–day period, it is important to put *understanding* and *sensitivity* into the hand/face/ball *relationship*. With each repositioning repetition, exercise your imagination of face/ball direction. When you do this, you make your mind commands and ball control one and the same. Play with the idea of various sizes and types of balls being struck by various sizes and shapes of flat–surfaced instruments. The physics remain constant.

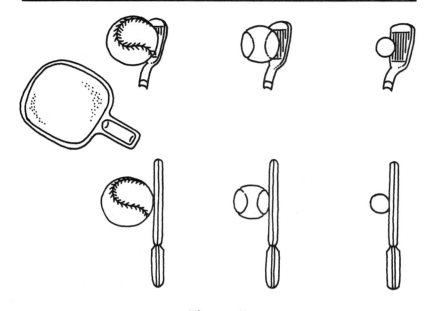

Figure 7

Improve you grip with the four–step approach. Each day for 21 days do the following:

1. Do the exercise in figure 4.
2. Repeat 60 times a day.
3. Evaluate only the content of the practice.
4. Have fun.
5. Exercise your imagination with ball/club/hands.

Two things are extremely important. First, you must do this exercise for 21 consecutive days. It will take less than five minutes a day. Keep a couple of clubs someplace where you can get at them easily. Each time you see a club, pick it up, position your hands, and reflect on the hands/clubface relationship. Second, once you have mastered this exercise, **GRADUATE** and go on to something else.

Your hand position of Vs aligned to your right ear and shoulder is a basic starting position. You will find that this position can and should be modified to spin the ball in a given direction. A slice spin will spin the ball clockwise. A hook spin will spin it counter–clockwise.

The spin of the ball depends on your physical structure, strength, and shot preference (spin preference) for the target

Figure 8

conditions. You can move the Vs to the right so that they point to the right of your shoulder. This increases clubface rotation during your forward swing, producing a hook spin, and the ball spins counter clockwise, resulting in a hook or draw. When you move the Vs to the left so that they point at your right eye or your nose, you decrease clubface rotation during your forward swing, and the ball spins clockwise.

Figure 9

After your initial 21–day habit–forming period, experiment freely and experience the various rotation factors and different positions. Keep in mind that you need to practice for 21 days and then graduate. Always remember that:

Hands and clubface are one–half of ball direction!

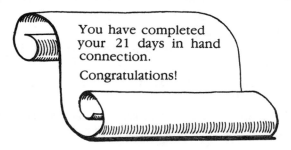

You have completed your 21 days in hand connection.

Congratulations!

Posture

The posture you assume in preparation is very important as it has tremendous influence on club path. Here is a simple rule to remember:

Hands are the face.
Posture is the path.

It's very simple. You are standing upright and have positioned your hands on the club. Your spine is vertical and your knees are straight.

Figure 10

Now, tilt your spine forward from your hips and tailbone (not from your waist). Flex your knees enough to feel spring, balance and readiness in your legs. Let your arms hang freely away from your abdomen, with your hands four to eight inches from your thighs.

You will notice that:

Your spine is still straight even though it is tilted forward.

Your shoulders and hips are counter-balanced to keep you from falling forward.

You feel light. This is the ready position of almost all sports.

Figure 11

Remember that spine tilt is critical to the swing concept.

At first all this may seem artificial because of the intellectual effort. Practice without a club for two or three days until you are extremely comfortable. Practice in front of the mirror until the image in the mirror and the image in your mind are one.

Figure 12

Now with the club in hand, tilt, flex, and lower the club to the ground. Your body position should remain constant and relaxed. Your left arm is reasonably straight, your right elbow is bent, and your right arm is relaxed. Your right shoulder is closer to the ground then your left.

Repeat this 60 times per day for 21 consecutive days.

The bottom of the clubhead (the sole) should be resting nearly flat on the ground, as shown in figure 13. If it is not, you may wish to have your clubs altered. The club can be bent (altered) so that the lie angle is proper for you. When the lie angle is proper for you, the length of the shaft can be shortened or lengthened to fit you properly. If you are a purely recreational golfer, you may not want to incur the expense of custom alterations to your clubs.

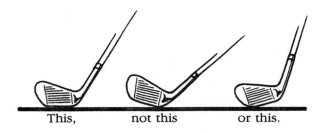

This,   not this   or this.

Figure 13

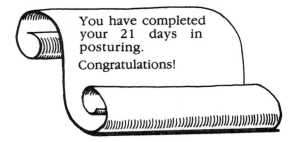

You have completed your 21 days in posturing.
Congratulations!

Positioning of the Ball

Position the ball so that when you are standing, the clubhead is squarely in front of your chest. When you tilt, flex, and lower the club to the ground, the clubhead will be positioned squarely between your feet. Your feet should be spaced at the width of your shoulders or slightly narrower.

Therefore, the *basic* ball position is:

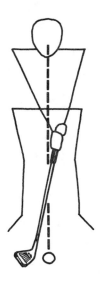

Figure 14

The ball is squarely between your feet, in front of your chest, under your nose.

Use this position for short and middle irons. For long irons and woods, position your body so the ball is in front of your left heel or left armpit.

Practice 21 days with intention and attention until this becomes a habit. Once you have learned this basic positioning, you can move the ball forward or back to create higher or lower trajectory shots to fit the conditions of the target. A higher trajectory is created by positioning the ball forward in your stance. A lower trajectory is created by positioning the ball back in your stance.

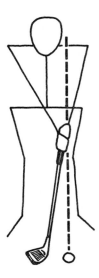

Figure   15

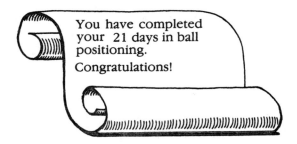

Alignment (Aim)

If left to your own devices, you know how to aim. Remember two things. First, the clubface should fundamentally be aimed with the flat surface perpendicular to the target. In some extreme conditions, the clubface might not aim at the target, for instance, when a tree or other obstacle is immediately in front of your line to the target.

Figure 16

This face to target relationship is fundamental, whether the club is elevated or soled on the ground.

Figure 17

Practice, recognize, and understand this basic concept of golf or any other flat surface striking game.

Second, the most important part of your body alignment is your shoulder alignment, not your feet.

Figure 18

The lines of your hips, knees, and feet should be parallel to your shoulders and they should aim in the same direction as your shoulders.

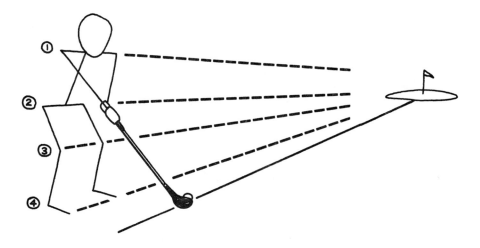

Figure   19

Remember that your body position is responsible for club-path. The path of the club will correspond to the direction of your shoulders first, your hips second, your knees third, and your feet last. This makes sense when you look at how your body is hooked together. Your arms are connected to your shoulders, not to your feet! Obviously, the alignment of your shoulders has the greatest effect on your arms and, therefore, on clubpath. The path of the club follows the line of your shoulders long before it follows the line of your feet.

Imagine a reference line from the ball straight to the target. Align the clubface perpendicular to this reference line. Now align your body lines — first your shoulders, then hips, then knees, and finally feet (toes) — parallel or slightly to the left of the line. The clubface is perpendicular to the reference line and therefore perpendicular to your body lines as long as your body matches the target line. Any deviation from this position of your body lines can only be slightly to the left of the reference line, but the clubface must remain fundamentally perpendicular to the target.

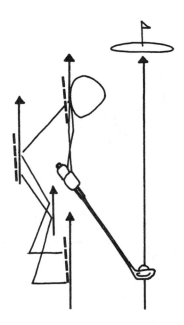

Figure 20

Practice alignment (aim) for 21 days with 60 repetitions a day. Use full intention and attention so that you form a good habit. Practice in your living room, backyard, a playground, or a driving range. Use a reference line on the ground to place the clubface perpendicular to the target and your shoulder lines slightly left of or parallel to the reference line.

An excellent way to check and validate alignment is to aim into a full-length mirror or window. Imagine the target or place a piece of tape in the center of the glass at shoulder height. Aim at the spot, then rotate your head and check your alignment by seeing your reflection.

After 21 days you can be assured that alignment is habituated, but you can easily monitor it if you wish. All you have to do is lay a club on the ground. Lay the club so that it lies on the reference line to the target, then turn your shoulders and body so that you are aligned parallel or slightly to the left of this line. Any time you practice on the driving range, you should follow this procedure.

Figure 21

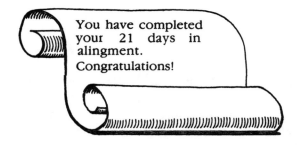

You have completed
your 21 days in
alingment.
Congratulations!

Routine Approach to the Ball

The final mechanical preparation is the formation of a routine approach to the ball. This is entirely personal because it is based on your internal pacing. This routine includes these six steps:

1. Gather information regarding the task at hand.
2. Mentally rehearse shot execution.
3. Approach and position the ball.
4. Align and aim.
5. Take a final waggle both internally and physically.
6. Relax and energize the motion of the swing through to acute awareness of target processing.

At first this routine may be slow and arduous; however, the fact that you have already satisfied the prerequisites of grip, aim, and alignment through habituation will make the routine quite easy to habituate. Your real obligation at this point is to become a gatherer of information about the target, to refine the information and react.

It is essential that you do this routine at your own rate and pace. Do not imitate other golfers, regardless of their skill level. You must develop this skill at your own rate because you may need 30 days, 90 days, 120 days or even longer to integrate your routine fully into your internal time clock. This synchronization process requires patience and repetition.

Start with awareness of the time it takes you to prepare for motion. As you become more comfortable, your attention will shift to the target. By the time it is routine, all preswing awareness will have been absorbed by the intensity of target awareness.

While it's easy to overlook or abbreviate the steps in an approach routine, if you do, you'll retard some of your future improvement. Eventually, compensations during swing must be attempted because of preswing failures. One compensation leads to another until you are hopelessly lost. If the score is important, and continued reduction in score is important, then the preswing mechanics are the foundation of any future improvement.

Everyone is anxious to hit the ball. It's fun, exhilarating and challenging. It can be a game unto itself. You do not need good physical mechanics to the hit the ball or to have fun attempting to do so. There is no rule that says you must play well to enjoy yourself. On the other hand, if you understand and absorb preswing functions, you can have the fun of hitting the ball, and you can enter the creative level where improvement is limitless.

You have completed your 21 days in ball approach.
Congratulations!

The Golf Swing

The only master model of the golf swing is the design of the club. This gives rise to four important key truths about the golf swing:

1. The golf swing is a *concept*, not a bunch of individual, independent things to do.
2. The greatest failure of most golf instruction is the use of the human element as the basis of swing theory.
3. The design of the golf club is the only legitimate master model for swing mechanics.
4. The golfer who fully grasps the intention of club design will swing in compliance with that understanding. Body movement will symptomatically fall into place.

So what is a golf club made to do? Well, in the days of the Romans or at least in the age of Mary, Queen of Scots, the *gawf* club was a hockey stick contraption made to hit a projectile some distance with some accuracy.

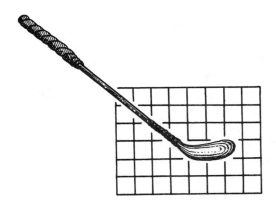

Figure 22

A hockey stick or ancient golf club has a design that gives about equal consideration of distance and direction of the puck or ball. The lie angle of both is about half way between vertical and horizontal, about 45 degrees.

Making the club lie that way made sense because original courses were short in yardage and the target may have been a larger area than today's small hole. Course conditions were rough, manicuring non–existent. Accuracy was as much by accident as by design. The flat lie–angle of the club reflected the somewhat random nature of the game.

Figure 23

Imagine the power that could be generated with a 180–inch club. You could hit a ball a mile if you could make accurate contact. But, while distance increases with club length, accuracy decreases. Even with accurate contact, the control direction with such a long club would be haphazard. If they had been playing a very short course, the control of direction might be at a premium, and great distance would not be needed. The club would be very short and lie–angle very upright.

Figure 24

This design would hit the ball very accurately but a very short distance compared with the 180–inch club.

As golf and golf courses evolved, clubs with various lie angles and lengths were needed to accomplish the various tasks demanded for accuracy or distance.

For example, of all the clubs, the driver (#1 wood) is designed for maximum distance and minimum direction control. There is not much loft on the clubface so the ball will have a relatively low flight trajectory, will hit the ground and roll a maximum distance. More to the point, the driver is the longest club, has the flattest lie angle, and is the hardest to hit accurately.

Figure 25

The putter is the exact opposite. A much shorter club, with an upright lie angle, it produces great accuracy. All the clubs between putter and driver are made to specialize in their own distance/direction compromise. Look at your clubs; you will see that the clubs with more vertical lie angles are shorter and have more loft to the clubface. This means that they can be used for higher, shorter, and more accurate shots.

Figure 26

Clubs with a flatter lie angle have to have a longer shaft or they wouldn't reach your hands. These clubs deliver greater clubhead speed and more distance.

Figure 27

As you can see, club design is a total concept. Longer clubs mean longer shots with less accuracy. Shorter clubs mean shorter shots with more accuracy.

Lie Angle

Club design, or lie angle, determines how a club is supposed to be swung. The lie angle of the club is clearly the only determining factor for the proper swing plane. When a golf ball is struck, it will initially move in compliance with the direction of the club's path at impact. The ball will then spin (curve) right, left, or straight, complying with the direction of the clubface at impact. This is true for the spin of any ball when struck by a flat surface. Take the time to ingest and digest this concept into every fiber of your being. Scrutinize all future instruction in light of these facts.

A putter and a driver are not designed to be swung the
same way. Neither are a nine iron and three iron. Two different lie angles dictate two different swing paths or swing
planes.

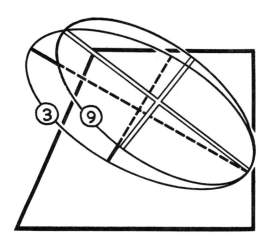

Figure 28

To get a feeling for what I mean, look at the swing path of
two different striking instruments: a baseball bat and a croquet mallet. A baseball bat is made to be swung horizontally
because the concept of the game is horizontal. The strike
zone demands that the ball be delivered to an area where the
bat must swing nearly horizontal with the ground to hit the
ball. Conceptually a horizontal swing plane is very flat. If you
play baseball, you swing according to your understanding of
that concept. A croquet mallet is made to be swung vertical-
ly. The hitting surface of the mallet is perpendicular to the
swinging surface. You must swing the mallet in a vertical
swing to play croquet because the concept of your game is
vertical. Obviously, you can't use a croquet mallet to play
baseball, and it is difficult to play croquet with a baseball bat.
Neither can be successful by design and concept.

Let's look again at the different lie angles of golf clubs.
Conceptually and functionally doesn't this mean that a different lie angle demands a different swing angle and swing
plane?

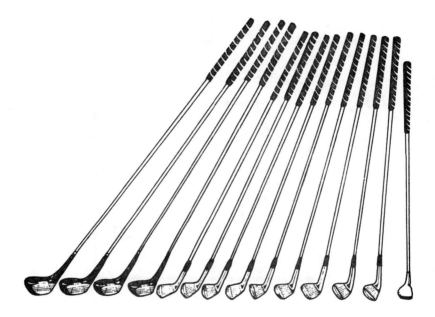

Figure 29

A three wood at the lie angle shown in figure 30 has a different swing plane built into it than a nine iron with the lie angle in figure 30.

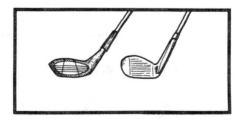

Figure 30

By design, the three wood must swing at a flatter (more horizontal) swing plane because of a flatter lie angle than the more upright nine iron. This is the reason that woods are not divot takers, and short irons take a divot. You can see that the flatter swing of the three wood dictated a sweeping motion of the clubhead. This motion will not be a divot taker. The steeper arc of the nine iron is a divot taker.

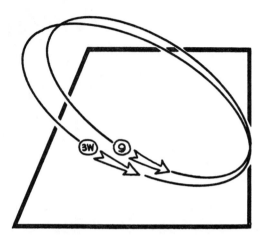

Figure 31

Club manufacturers test golf equipment with mechanical hitting machines. These machines swing the club perfectly because each club is swung on its designed swing plane corresponding to the lie angle.

The club is clamped into the gripping device at a horizontal level.

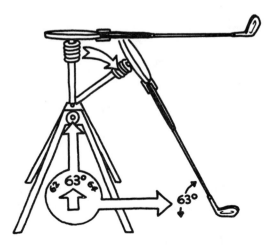

Figure 32

The proper swing plane is then dialed into the machine. For each club put into the machine a new number must be dialed. This number is found by measuring the lie angle of the club to be tested.

You can see that if an adjustment were not made in the machine's setting after the club was changed, the club wouldn't hit the ball correctly. For example, the driver has the most horizontal swing plane because of its horizontal lie angle.

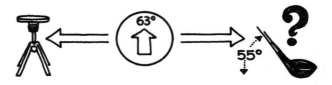

Figure 33

If the machine were reloaded with an eight iron but the operator forgot to adjust the machine setting corresponding to the new lie angle, the ball would never be hit. Consider the disastrous consequences of loading a driver into a eight iron setting. The consequences are just as disastrous if you misload your swing in the same way. Think about this before you look at the picture.

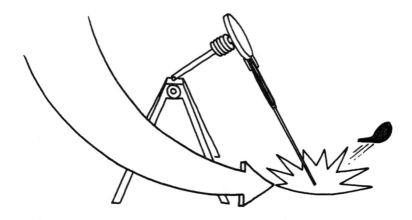

Figure 34

Let's go one step further. Imagine that you are holding a club 50 feet long. What would the lie angle of a club this long be? Imagine addressing the ball, soling the club behind a ball 50 feet from you. Now imagine the swing plane appropriate for this club. Repeat this swing plane over and over until you can really feel the baseball–bat–like motion. Close your eyes and imagine this entire process.

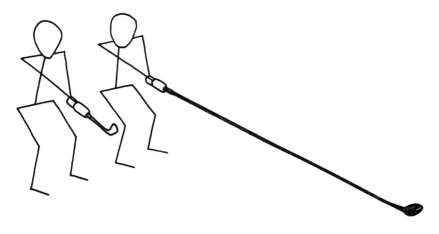

Figure 35

Now, change clubs. Your new club is two feet long. What is the lie angle? Address the ball and repeat a number of these vertical swing planes. As a final test, feel yourself swinging the two–foot club on the same plane as the fifty foot club. Sillier yet, try the 50 foot club on the same swing plane as the two foot club. Did you have to use a ladder, or did you legs grow an extra 45 feet or so? This recognition of different lie angles destroys the traditional idea that every club should be swung the same.

Hit the Ball Straight?

Another concept about golf swing can be equally disturbing. You may have been told to hit the ball straight, or straight back and through. This concept implies that all clubs have a vertical swing plane associated with an upright or vertical lie angle such as a putter or a croquet mallet. Let's go back to the manufacturer's mechanical hitting machine. When the proper swing plane is dialed into the machine, the vertical arm of the machine tilts forward (like your spine) until the prescribed tilt is reached and the club is soled flat on the ground. Presto! The club is mechanically swung in a circular motion. The circle is tilted on a perfect plane for that club. The machine follows an arc. The club is *not* swung straight back through relative to the reference line to the target. Golf clubs are designed to be swung in a prescribed arc.

The word **straight** should be eliminated from the concept of a golf swing. *Throw **straight** out of your golf vocabulary and your golfing concept.* In fact, use the term *target line* with caution. The fact that a reference line from the ball to the hole or target is a necessity for body alignment and clubface aim does not imply that the ball should be struck in a perfectly straight line every time.

All golf clubs are designed to travel on a path that is circular, meeting the reference line at only one tangent point. The ball is the point of the tangent.

When you understand the concept of a flatter swing plane, the longer clubs, two and three irons, fairway woods, and drivers will all be much easier to hit proficiently. Most golfers have a terrible time with striking long clubs because concep-

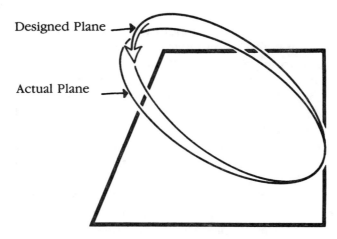

Designed Plane

Actual Plane

Figure 36

tually they have tried to swing them at the more upright swing plane designed for seven, eight and nine irons. They have not used the concept of the flatter swing plane. This is not unlike trying to swing the fifty foot club on the same plane as the two foot club. As your mind accepts the concept of a flatter swing plane the game becomes easier and your scores go down.

Actually, golf clubs are designed so that the proper mistake is to swing the club on a flatter plane than the club is design-ed for rather than a more upright plane.

While it may, at first, seem unreasonable to consider mak-ing a mistake during the golf swing, especially an intentional mistake of swinging too flat; the fact is that you are a human being and you occasionally make errors. It is better to make a tolerable error which is within the confines of club design than to violate the design of the lie angle with a swing that is too upright.

Swing Plane

The two most important things that you need to remember are:

Swing plane is the most important consideration of your swing.
Your hands are reactive to the path of the club.

Your mind is so incredibly efficient that survival instincts will take corrective and instantaneous adjustments in club-face alignment during your forward swing of the club. These survival instincts will be of great benefit to scoring efficiency when the path of the club is consistently on one plane.

If the plane is slightly flat, there are two benefits derived. First, the path is within the club design function. Second, your subtle mind recognizes this consistency and discharges commands to your hands/clubface to operate the face con-sistently in relation to the target. If the human element fluc-tuates in swing path errors — too vertical, then too flat and then too vertical, then too flat — the survival instincts are overloaded. Your brain's message is confused about which swing path is coming up and the corrective face angle mechanism becomes jumbled. A consistent *mistake* turns out to be no mistake at all.

Swing Inside Out

This entire swing concept boils down to one simple idea: *swing insideout.*

If you have followed the idea of lie angle/swing path closely, you know that ten different golf clubs with ten different lie angles demand ten different swing planes or paths.

But it would be hopelessly complicated actually to do this, so we must find the common denominator of club design, a single element that is simple and repeatable.

All golf clubs are designed to swing from inside toward outside.

The club must be swung inside toward the outside of the reference line.

The golf club must be swung inside–out of the reference line. The reference line is a line parallel to your shoulder line

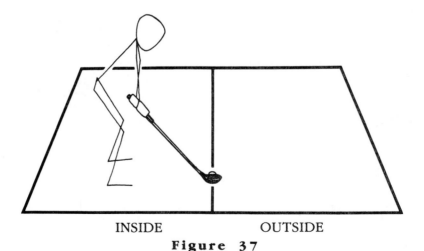

INSIDE   OUTSIDE

Figure 37

which intersects the ball. While the reference line can be identical to the target line, they are not the same thing. They are not always identical or even parallel. For example, you might be in a situation where there is a tree between you and the target. The reference line goes to one side of the tree or the other.

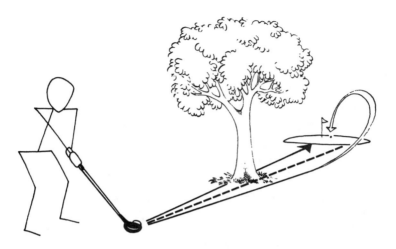

Figure 38

Use the reference line to align your body for a shot. Remember that it is a line parallel to your shoulders that intersects the ball. Here is a little exercise that shows you the

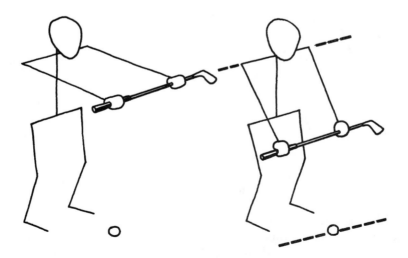

Figure 39

reference line. First, put a ball or some other small object on the ground, about two feet in front of your toes. Next, pick up a club or other straight object and hold it straight out from your shoulders, parallel to the ground. Hold it with both hands. Your hands should be about two feet apart. Now, keeping your elbows locked and straight, lower your arms until the clubshaft is in a line between your eyes and the ball. The reference line is now on the ground, defining the aim of your body.

The entire area on your side of the reference line is _inside_. The entire area on the other side is _outside_. All golf clubs are designed to swing inside toward outside during the _forward_ swing.

The line from the ball to the target is your target line. You align and aim your body on the reference line.

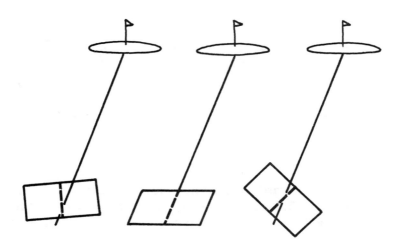

Figure 40

The club's path must always swing inside toward out of the reference line but not _necessarily_ of the target line. This ties into the golf club as the master model of the swing. Imagine that you are elevated directly above the hitting machine, looking straight down at the center of the machine. Do you see the eliptical shape of the club path?

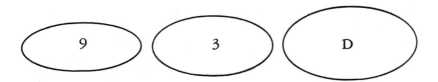

Figure 41

Do you see that as the lie angle of the club gets flatter, the shaft gets longer, and the shape of the path is less elipitical and more circular? Now, look at yourself from the same perspective. Introduce the reference line, parallel to your shoulders, intersecting the ball. Do you see the path of the clubhead moving inside toward outside during the forward swing? Do you see the clubhead moving out and away from you during the forward swing?

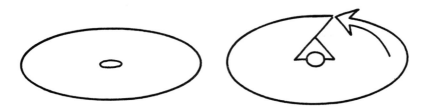

Figure 42

During the forward swing, the club must move inside toward outside. The forward swing is the *only* time it counts. Remember the basic premise, only the club hits the ball. The

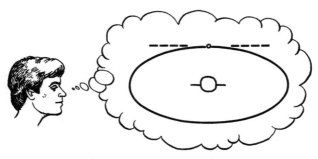

Figure 43

ball never responds to you. The ball's destination is a function of face, path, and velocity. The only time the ball gets hit is on the forward swing.

One reason golf is such a deceptive athletic motion is because it is difficult for the untrained observer to see great players change the direction of the path from backswing to the forward swing. Jack Nicklaus, Tom Watson, and, most dramatically, Isao Aoki move the club back on a very vertical swing plane (violating club design) but reroute the club into proper (designed) plane path on the forward swing. These players hit wonderful shots because the design function of the golf club is satisfied on the forward swing when, and only when, the golf ball is struck.

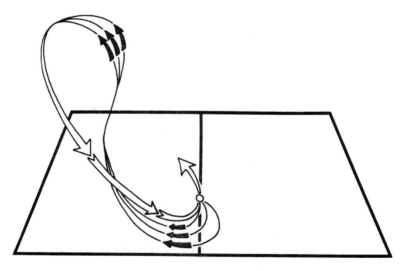

Figure 44

More on Inside Toward Outside

The inside toward outside swing is exactly the same process as that of a mechanical batting device. You have become the mechanism. You will swing according to the concept you have implanted. Your mind/body has no choice!

This inside toward outside swing is a mechanically perfect swing. After the club passes through the ball (the outermost tangent to the arc), the clubpath returns back inside. So the proper term for the *perfect* swing (the perfect plane for the lie angle) is actually inside to inside. Unfortunately the human mechanism is not perfect. As such, the proper and preferred mistake to make is to make the swing plane too flat rather than too upright during the forward swing.

The reason that the upright plane is such a scoring disaster is that the clubpath travels *outside* toward *inside* during the forward swing. This is clearly a gross violation of golf club design.

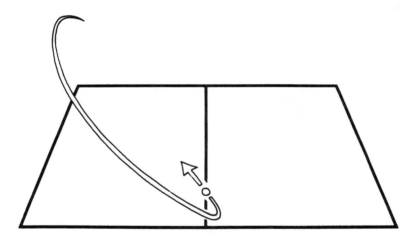

Figure   45

Let's make the proper mistake — swing inside out.

This is easy to accomplish. It is a by–product of making the forward swing flatter than the design of the club.

This is the final and complete conclusion to a swing concept which will always keep the golf club functioning within design limitations. At this point you should repeat the intellectual and intuitive exercises in figure 39. They will help you reinforce and understand this concept. If scoring is important to you, do not **graduate** to golfing until you accomplish this. (If scoring is not important to you, go play golf and have fun.)

As you are habituating the inside/outside golf swing through concept integration, you will align your body,

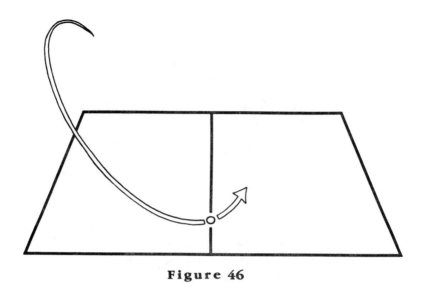

Figure 46

notably your shoulder line, in relation to the target line for the desired shot.

Lee Trevino has long understood this concept. This makes Trevino one of golf's all–time best ball strikers. Trevino's swing is severely inside/outside relative to body lines.

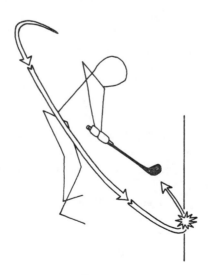

Figure 47

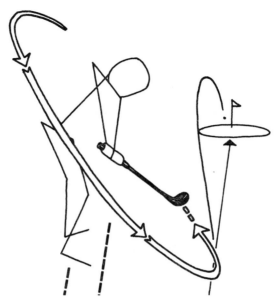

Aligning his body lines left of target, the
clubpath travels slightly outside–in of the
target line.

Figure 48

Trevino's ball flight pattern therefore is left to right of the
target line, right to right of his original body lines. The ball
must start left of the target line (even though he swings inside–out of body lines). His supreme internal awareness of
the target keeps the clubface square to the target, imparting a
mild clockwise spin on the ball.

Trevino also understands that the power of inside–out
swing combined with the control of fading ball spin is a maximum utility of club design. Do you understand that his shot
is left to right of target line, right to right of body lines?
Review this concept. Find the answer in concept, not as a
bunch of things to do.

Peter Jacobsen swings very mildly inside–out of his body
lines. He aligns very slightly, almost imperceptibly, left of the
target line. The clubpath travels down the target line an inor-
dinately long time. The clubface is square to the target or
very minutely open. The shot pattern is straight or very
slightly to right.

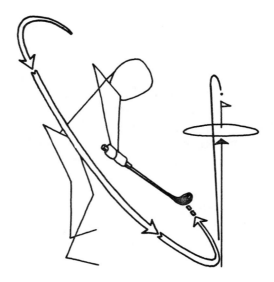

Figure 49

Many good touring players and low handicap amateurs move the ball from right to left. Gary Player swings inside–out of his body lines. His body lines correspond to the

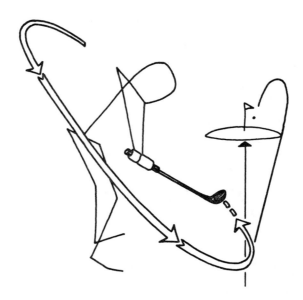

Figure 50

target line as he addresses the ball, so the path of the club is also inside–out of the target line. Target awareness demands that the clubface be square to the target (or minutely open) at impact, spinning the ball mildly counter clockwise, hooking the ball back into the target from its initial direction created by the path traveling right of target.

What is most evident is that all good players swing in-side–out of their body lines. By personal evolution or by conscious choice they position their body lines in relation to the target line to accommodate the type of shot (ball flight) pattern they choose to create. By strong target awareness, sheer intuition, and/or conceptual understanding, the club-face is square, open (right) or closed (left) of the path, creating the needed spin of the ball to get it close to the target.

The ball will always start its flight in the direction of the swing path and the curve according to the spin applied to the ball by the direction the clubface (hands) is pointing at impact.

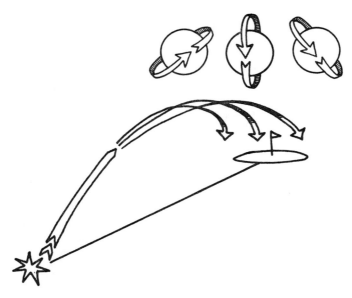

Figure 51

If you want to improve your score, you must make the conscious choice of an inside–out swing path to satisfy the design built into the club. This swing path must be an outgrowth of deeply felt conceptual understanding, if it is to be durable and consistent. No amount of individual independent tips, secrets, or fragmented things to do will accomplish the same goal.

The inside–out concept is extremely important. It is a swing error that is not an error. It permits a swing path consistent with the limitations of club design. The consistency of the path gives your subtle mind the opportunity to function with the clubface relative to the target. You have eliminated two of three clubhead paths and any confusion you have about clubface aim.

When the swing path is firmly conceived by your mind's eye and is combined with the sensitive connection of your hands to the club, you will have instant creativity and proficiency. Your mind will become connected to the target, free of cluttering thoughts regarding the swing, and open to process all the information coming through sensory receptors from the target. To the degree that you learn and practice the skills of trusting your image processing, you will play your best golf.

The golf swing must swing inside toward outside during the forward swing of the club. Here is an exercise that will help you remember this concept.

Swing Concept Exercise

The purpose of this exercise is to establish a clear sense of swing plane. Do not continue with this exercise or this chapter unless you understand that an inside toward outside swing plane is important during the forward swing. In addition, it must become obvious to you that an outside–in path is the worst possible violation of the design of the golf club. Consider now what would happen to the hitting machine if it were to swing outside–in. The machine would have to fall apart to do so.

Begin with the general relaxation exercise described in the introduction, then proceed.

1. Imagine the lie–angle of a 9 iron and the club soled flat on the ground and supporting itself.

2. Imagine a flat circle sitting on its edge and the same tilt as the 9 iron.
3. See yourself standing inside the circle preparing to execute a swing motion. You are fully aware that the attitude of the club shaft and circle are in exact alignment on the forward swing to, through and past the ball. If there is any error it is always under the circle during the forward swing.
4. Imagine a driver, its lie angle and corresponding circle. Swing accordingly.
5. Go through a number of clubs following the same sequence. Take practice swings. Hit balls. Hit practice shots on the course. At all times, see and feel the motion of your arms and the club-shaft/clubhead on the appropriate swing plane. The occasional and intentional error will be to deliver the clubhead to the ball under the circle, flatter than prescribed by the lie angle of the club.

Practice frequently and thoroughly. Make sure you feel the swing in all positions while you also feel relaxation, rhythm, and complete balance.

You may wish to actually sole various clubs. Lean them against the back of a chair and sit facing the club as if you were the target. This can help you imagine the circular swing plane. Alternate and study each club as you develop subtle feels for each one in turn.

Be Task Oriented

All great golfers and other great athletes find themselves in their vocations because of an intuitive trust of task orientation. Many professional golfers may fall from the grace of this state of trust. They may lack the deep conceptual understanding of proper swing concept even though they initially performed the swing properly through imitation and repetition. When trust breaks down, however, the search for a way back destroys more careers than it makes.

The personal stories of hundreds of players are very similar to the dilemma of the average amateur golfer. The advice, tips, and an enormously wide range of personal opinions you can get are endless. You will find your mind dwelling on self–oriented mechanics and therefore cut yourself off from target awareness and the opportunity to create from the vast potential of your mind the appropriate response to the target. The cycle is vicious. The more intense the mechanical search becomes, the less target–oriented your mind becomes. Self–trust rapidly diminishes. Self distrust spawns a greater mechanical search, less target awareness, and the cycle continues.

Although this book is primarily concerned with your ability to identify, intensify, and manage your internal image–making process, I recognize that the fundamentals of a golfing education are a necessity. Target awareness, the source of creativity and trust, must be supported by the intellectual and conceptual *pre–golf course* strategies.

The answers to mechanical breakdown can always be found and remedied very quickly by checking the intellectual area of preswing or the conceptual area of swing. Most often, it is grip, stance/posture, aim/alignment, or the routine approach to the ball. The faulty area is almost always an extension of inadequate habit formation during the initial learning or relearning sequence. When you find the troublesome area, assign it to a 21–day period of practice in which you give it full attention and intention during each repetition. Whether the correction lies in preswing activity or in swing function, it must be addressed and remedied during practice, not during play.

If you find that the problem is a lack of clarity regarding the concept of club design, and the demand of an inside–out path, then you must interna'ize the concept more deeply. Commit yourself purely to the mental exercises available in this book. They will more firmly etch into your mind the use of the golf club as it is designed. You will find the design factor simple and straightforward. As your understanding of club design improves, your game will improve naturally. Be sure to do the exercises outlined in this chapter and commit 21 days to each improvement you would like to make. You'll learn to play the game better and enjoy it more.

Whether the remedy lies in preswing activity or in swing function, it must be remedied off the golf course. This course is for liberation of the fantastic potential of the human mind. The golf course is for the absorption of the target and its conditions and your reaction to it. It is an ongoing exercise in creativity and self–trust.

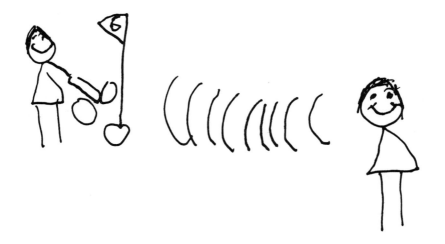

Hannah Hogan's *Imaging Golf*, age 5, July 3, 1985

Day 3

What Is An Image?

" . . . A vivid image appeared in my mind's eye, of a turquoise ball traveling down the right side of the fairway with a tail hook toward the green. I took my stance and waggled the club carefully, aware that the image of the shot was incredibly vivid. Then I swung and the ball followed the path laid in my mind."

from *Golf in the Kingdom*
by Michael Murphy

What is an image? It's your thought, your reality, or anything you want it to be. It is the language your body understands. Every action you make is stimulated by an image. If you decide to turn on the lamp by your chair and then reach out to turn the knob or pull the chain, you have done so through imagery. Remember that your brain processes about 10,000 bits of information per second, whether you're aware of it or not. Obviously there is a great deal of processing that happens that you do not notice. Your arm is able to reach out for the lamp because your brain has sent out an image-a series of signals, patterns that your arm responds to. Remember, too, that your mouth speaks about two words per second. That means that approximately 9,998 pieces of information pass through your brain per second that you are not paying attention to while you are speaking. Your speaking, by the way, includes your internal dialogue or self–talk as well as what you say out loud.

There are many types of images you use continuously. In your image practice, the menu you can choose from is varied, and you have ample opportunity to keep yourself interested. It's a lot like eating pizza. I love pizza. Chicago–style, double sauce, double cheese. Yet if I were told that I could have only pizza for every meal for the rest of my life, it would take about four days before I could never look another tomato in the eye . The same is true for your golf game. Your images are your ingredients, and you are at your best golf game when you are in the image kitchen without measuring spoons or recipe books.

Types of Imagery

Here are some types of imagery you are likely to use in your golf game. As you look at this list, you will gravitate towards some types as ones you use naturally. You have already found them to be effective for you on the course. Others will seem, perhaps, silly or out of line for your personality and game. Every individual is different, and you are your own best judge about which images make the most sense for you. Start with and concentrate on those that are clearest to you, that you find easiest to trust, and those that your body tends to respond to efficiently. Practice and indulge yourself in all types of images. This will increase your flexibility, and you will have more fun.

TYPE	EXAMPLE
General	"I'm a good putter"
End-result (being there)	"I can see/feel/smell that the ball is in the hole "
Process (getting there)	"I can sense the ball sliding down a silver trough to go into the hole"
Induced	"Hey Charlie — do you ever duck hook on this hole?"
Spontaneous	"I know I'm gonna make this!"
Concrete	"The putter face strikes the ball and it slams into the back right corner of the cup"
Symbolic	"I've got a 30 foot snake here" or "This putter is a brush and I'll just paint–stroke this ball in the hole"

There are other types of images that you are very familiar with. Dreams, daydreams, and fantasies are all image states. They are often very vivid and engaging. Although you may not remember your dreams, you certainly have times when you have a definite quality of emotion and sense of impact from a dream. The moments right before you fall asleep and just as you are waking are wonderfully rich times for you to observe your images. Your daydreams and fantasies are often pleasant distractions from your daily routine, and you may notice the next time you find yourself daydreaming that you feel refreshed from your mental excursion. That quality of refreshment is a physiological by–product of imaging and reduces stress and tension in your body. Start nurturing these image states by paying more attention to them as they occur. This will help support your development in creating specific images for your mental golf practice and play.

Still other types of images that you are familiar with are in your memory and imagination. Can you remember a favorite round of golf? Can you remember your bedroom as a little child? Can you imagine a golf course on the moon? Can you imagine a course composed of all the holes where you've played your greatest golf? As you gaze into your mind to answer these questions, please understand that your responses are all in images. This is a good time to ask you to rally all of your senses to provide you with a vivid and detail-ed image. For instance, imagining the golf course on the moon will probably lead you into a sense of weightlessness. This is a valid kinesthetic image; in fact it is essential when considering the atmosphere on the moon and how you would picture the experience of playing a round up there. As an aside, take a moment and remember a favorite song from your days in high school. Doesn't the memory of that song usher in a flood of various images of your high school sweetheart, a football season, a moody evening in late September? Your sense of hearing is very important in pain-ting a full *picture* of a memory image. So be sure not to limit your image building to the visual. Your golfing images will fill out just as these two examples of imagined and memory images are filled out with the inclusion of all of your senses.

There is also guided imagery. This is the type of imagery a hypnotist specializes in. You can guide your own images by determining a specific mode or sequence with which to approach a given task. Your routine approach to each shot is, in effect, a guided image. If you choose to approach a round of golf by deciding to engage actively in positive, affirming self–talk throughout the entire game then you have given yourself a general, guided image for that activity.

The eidetic image is the cream of the crop; it feels like a gift from heaven, and is a true joy to have and behold. It is an image that is extremely vivid, lucid, and real. Your body will never be confused when you have an eidetic image. The message through the neuro-pathways will be picture-perfect. Unique experiences of peak performance such as those presented by Michael Murphy and Rhea White in their book *The Psychic Side Of Sports*, are characterized by descriptions from athletes of perceptions and images which defy reality and yet were emphatically real. Those perceptions were eidetic images which clearly defined a special view of the task at hand and their role within it. Every dedicated professional and enthusiast experiences moments like these in their chosen endeavor. Trust yourself and your images, and you will increase their frequency in your game and life.

Practice Your Imagery Daily

Practice your imagery on a daily basis, and you will begin to enhance your ability to attach to and give life to your images . Importantly, you will begin to perceive your images as much a part of your life as tying your shoes. As you grow with your images, you can graduate to another level. No longer mental mechanics, they become pure creative responses which flourish under the attention and trust you give them. If you're saying to yourself that this sounds too hokey and oversimplified, just think about your intuition. How many times would you have given your eye–teeth to have the opportunity to replay a shot the way it first occurred to you? You knew which club to select, the distance, the feel, and then you doubted yourself, made other choices, and blew the shot. "If only I'd gone with my intuition, I know I could have made it. I just know it." Webster defines intuition as "direct knowing without the conscious use of reasoning." Our intuition lets us know so much more than we're aware. Our intuition presents itself as spontaneous images of all types, shapes, sizes, and colors. Noticing and trusting is the first step. You will become comfortable with your ability to create and trust images as you build a track record of patient, curious, and persistent practice.

There is another distinction I would like to make about images and the way you process them. The information you gather from the outside world through your senses is processed in your brain as images. You gather information with your eyes, ears, nose, taste buds, hands, and skin. Everybody has at least one sensory dominance. Mine is visual. This means that as I gather information for a shot, I rely on and most trust the information conveyed by my eyes to my brain. Once the information is processed, however, I *feel* the shot I need to make in response to the information I have gathered . The image I attach to for shot creation is primarily kinesthetic. Coming in, I'm visual; going out, I'm kinesthetic. In contrast, both Johnny Miller and Peter Jacobsen are cross–dominant in their own unique ways. Johnny Miller relies on both visual and kinesthetic information going in and kinesthetic going out. Peter Jacobsen is visual coming in and appears to rely on both visual and kinesthetic going out.

What are you? Your practice and notes will reveal this answer over time. Your intuition will be the best place to start, but do realize that Western culture is very biased towards visual. Current research indicates that 60 percent of Westerners tested are visually dominant. That research does not make a distinction between information being processed going in or going out. If you've always considered yourself poor at visualization, you may be in the 40 percent of the people who are not visually oriented.

Take your time with this issue. Don't be too quick to come to conclusions. The intent is for you to learn what sensory mode or modes will best get your image rheostat to deliver a 100 percent charge from neurons in your brain to muscles in your body. Just remember that your image building does have these two major steps: images that occur from gathering information, and images that occur in response to that information. The process can happen during the blink of an eye or over the course of a few seconds. It certainly happens faster than you can talk about it, so you will want to give yourself plenty of time to observe and determine what your leading sense is.

Image practice is simple to do. The hardest part is taking time to do it. One thing for sure is that you need to make it fun. You want to look forward to it. If it isn't fun, either you won't do it or, when you do drag yourself into a practice session convinced that it won't be fun, it won't be of benefit to you. If you have a type A personality you may find it much easier to spend three hours on the driving range during a blizzard than to take 15 minutes on the living room couch imaging your way around the golf course. That step, obviously, is yours to take when you are ready. Look at it this way: what have you got to lose? Monitoring your levels of tension and stress, both physical and mental, makes a significant contribution to your state of well–being. The process of imaging has been proven to relax and rejuvenate your mind and body. Images are a safety release valve for stress. In addition, imaging has been demonstrated to have a significant effect on the outcome of a player's golf shots. Reduced stress and improved golf shots give you twice the bonus value generated from your time spent.

You Are a Pioneer

Your decision to do this automatically qualifies you as a pioneer. I say this because there is no support system already created for you to lean on and make use of. You will be your own ice–breaker as you forge your way into a new relationship with the likes of your spouse and playing partners. An astronaut has an extensive crew of life support people. You are the only life support system your image life has. Your spouse may think you're crazy to lie down on the couch and build swing planes. Your playing partners can't be expected to understand you when you yell "YEAH! WHAT A GREAT IMAGE. I THOUGHT SAND AND THE BALL IS IN THE BUNKER!" for a double bogey. You're pioneering new territory in your mind. What sets you apart from Lewis and Clark is that you can turn back if you don't like what you find, whereas their only choice was to take it all in, respond to their best advantage, and keep heading for the Pacific Ocean. In some ways, your ability to choose not to continue your image trek makes your journey harder. Your commitment will be reaffirmed frequently in the face of a high score or a series of duck hooks that you're sure you didn't image. Yet you always do get what you think.

The desire to practice imagery and improve your control over your images is the most important key. Over the last few years, there have been several groups of people who have had four hours of training and then walked over hot coals. These novice fire walkers were people who were interested in demonstrating to themselves how powerful their images were. One of our instructors participated and reported that he kept himself very relaxed and imagined the he was walking over a layer of ice cubes. The physiological response of his body complied with his image, and his feet did not blister. The August 15, 1985 *Salt Lake Tribune* reported that the coach of the University of Hawaii football team had many of his players walk over the coals. Unfortunately, the title of the article was "Mind over Matter." It might have been more appropriately named "Mind is Matter."

Again I remind you that you have graduated from Mrs. Compton's typing class. Leave the typewriter in the closet, put on your golf shoes, and tell a story for each shot. Your trek through 18 holes may not receive the recognition Lewis and Clark did, but your golf game will be much more fun.

Some Rules of Imagery

1. **Be kind to yourself.** Give yourself the opportunity to grow within this new approach. Don't expect to be a Picasso when you've just bought your first set of watercolors.

2. **Don't try; let it happen.** Whenever you try, it is a sure sign that you are on the outside looking in. You are separated from the experience by trying to get into it. You are better off to INTUIT.

3. **Whatever images occur are appropriate for you at the time.**

4. **The more you commit to image practice, the greater the value it will have in your life and your golf game.** One of the reasons imagery is so useful for people who are ill is that they really have a need for it. When faced with life or death situations, people really need to make a commitment. Golf is not life or death even though it seems to be for a lot of people. Your images *are* the life of your golf game. Why not commit to them?

5. **Be kind to yourself.** This is not a misprint. This is simply a very important concept that I want you to absorb, and I think it merits repetition.

Strategies of Mental Imagery Practice

Determine what time of day is the best for you to set aside as quiet time. Ask yourself what time of day you would want to take a battery of college exams. This will be your time for imaging and relaxation practicing. Start with an expectation that you know you can fulfill. Five minutes that drifts into ten is preferable to 30 minutes that peters out at ten. You don't need to saddle yourself with guilt. Two short sessions during a day may fit your personal style and work demands better than one longer one. Set a timer so that you don't have to concern yourself with whether you're going over your time limit or be worried about whether or not you may fall asleep. This frees up your brain from little constrictions and lets you put 100 percent into your session.

Keep a journal of your practice. Make notes of your images, the topics you select, the time of day you practice, the quality of your experience, etc. The journal will help you validate and support your progress. Experience is your best teacher.

Practice all types of images and all facets of the golf game. You will find that the imagery types are frequently mixed together. An image of a chip shot will often be a combination of both end–result and process. It may easily be either concrete or symbolic. You may find your images are spontaneous for one shot and that you need to induce them for the next. There is no right or wrong here. There is only an endless combination of image types and sensory images for you to draw from and engage in.

Practice general and specific images. Rehearse an entire round of golf. That's a general theme, and within it are several stories. One story per shot, and each shot is triggered by a specific image. With each shot, you take in and put out images. This is exactly like your breathing. You breathe in and you breathe out. These are two specific images which comprise the general image which is : *Yes, I'm breathing.* When you strike the ball, however, remember that the final image you project will dictate the reality of the shot you make. On the golf course, the end–result is the best image you can have at the final point of impact.

Beginning, Middle and End

This can be a tricky point, and I want to clarify it as best I can. Every shot has a beginning, a middle, and an end. Every shot starts with the club face being delivered to the ball. After the ball is struck or putted, there is the middle section of the shot. This is the time the ball is moving from Point A to Point B. The end of the shot is the target — where the ball finally comes to rest. If your body is to receive complete information about what you want the shot to do, you must fill out each of these three phases in your images. If any one of them is vague or incomplete, your body won't receive a complete message. This means that although your end and beginning may have stellar image quality, if the middle is muddled your shot may be less than stellar. This opens the door for frustration when you're actually on the course: you know that your image was great — so what happened? What happened was truly that at least one portion of the shot image you projected was not as great as you may have believed. Another possibility is that the images you gathered before you made the shot were somehow incomplete. For instance, perhaps you didn't notice the image of the wind direction and failed to include that in the ingredients when you developed the main course of the shot. Still another possibility is that physically you were too tense to respond to your images properly. Mental mechanics and images are subtle, and the time frame for each shot is a matter of seconds. This is a situation where you must follow the rule: **Be kind to yourself.**

When you're not actually on the course, practice the beginning, middle, and end of each shot you create while lying on your couch. Do several series of shots where you move mentally from end to middle to beginning. This will help to set up the feel that you are responding and reacting to the target with each shot you make. Image practice is free of consequences. It is a safe time for you to develop familiarity with imaging that allows you to build confidence in the process and in yourself. Obviously, this will transfer to your imaging while on the course.

Interestingly, you take in information by imaging the shot. The end of the shot gives you the details of the middle process of the shot and therefore directs the action needed for the beginning of the shot. You take in information, end, middle, beginning, and then put the shot out, beginning, middle, end. Think about it; isn't this how you play catch or hit a ping pong ball?

Pre-play the End Result

Let's look at other aspects of general or broad images. Pre-play the events that will follow a round. If you are competing for the city championship, rehearse your victory speech, imagine conversations with the press. Notice what the notoriety will do to your social schedule. Practice living with these results until they are comfortable. The advantage to this practice is two-fold. You have already rehearsed your acceptance speech so you don't have to shift your attention to that as you're on the 16th tee. That is a great advantage because it means that you will have attention for 100 percent wattage through the neuro-rheostat to your muscles for your tee shot. It is also a great advantage because you have given yourself the opportunity to exercise several of your senses as you construct your image of that speech. You see yourself walking up towards the trophy, you hear the host praise your victory, you feel the wind and sun on your arms, you moisten your lips as you notice that your mouth is dry from nervousness just as you begin to speak. You can smell the roses that decorate the awards table. All of the input from all of these modalities really fills in the *picture*, and your image becomes as real as if the experience were actually happening. Let this pre–round rehearsal benefit your general sense of well–being and confidence by giving it your full attention and trust.

Let's consider another option . Pre–play your post–round by imaging your response to losing the tournament. This does not mean that you're programming yourself for failure. It means you are giving yourself the opportunity to exercise your perceptual flexibility and turn the situation of losing to your advantage. This flexibility shows signs of great mental health. Peter Jacobsen demonstrated this beautifully during an interview after losing the 1985 Honda Classic to Curtis Strange in a play–off. When asked how he felt about missing the putt that cost him the victory he replied, "I didn't miss the putt; the ball missed the hole." Peter viewed the situation objectively and with a sense of humor. His attachment to the image of that putt was strong. He felt it was a vivid and clear image and that he had stroked the ball accordingly. In review, he judged the clarity and content of his image rather than the outcome of the putt. Pre–play a loss by seeing and feeling yourself as if you were an objective observer of the event. The value of this is that you will already have rehearsed it so that during an actual event you can draw upon memory images that guide you towards perceptual flexibility and away from physical tension and stress. If you're coming down 18, having just double bogied 17 to lose the lead, you will be able to give each remaining shot 100 percent which is the best you can do in that situation or in any situation, for that matter.

Thursday Afternoon Sound Session

At this point you may be saying to yourself, "What sort of things should I think about in an image session?". Here is what happened to one of my students.

Vin Hoover, a business executive and amateur golfer, attended an S.E.A. golf school at Saddlebrook in April of 1985.

He had an image session which centered on the frustrations he felt about doubt, fear, and nervousness. I include a transcription here to illustrate the use of symbolic images in dissolving dis–ease. It also illustrates that your sixth sense, the sense of humor, often plays a significant role in images.

In an earlier sound session, Vin pictured himself playing golf with Arnold Palmer and Jack Nicklaus at Grandfather Mountain in North Carolina. In this *game* Vin pictured both Arnold and Jack carrying his clubs after the fourth hole. He was so far ahead that they felt it was the only decent thing to do. In this session Vin starts out by wondering how he can take charge of his emotions, and then things get real interesting:

> People who have anguished over golf sometimes live in a hell. There has to be a way to end that hell and take away those emotions that encompass us as we play golf. My thoughts were, "Well, how will I best take charge of those emotions. If it is pure hell that overtakes me as I play golf, the first thing for me to do is to go underground and find out how I could, finally, take over those emotions."
>
> There were three emotions. Number one was Doubt, number two was Fear, and number three was Nervousness. As I went down through the tunnel in the ground, it reminded me of the old story of *Twenty Thousand Leagues Under the Sea.* As I was going down through deep, dark caverns, I knew that if I made the journey down into hell to get these emotions, I would, indeed, capture them. They knew it also, and as they knew it, they were running from me. They knew at this time that Doubt, Fear, and Nervousness were about to be had. And as I went through these caverns of . . . smell . . . and darkness . . . there seemed to be road blocks and they were kind of flashing signs at me . . . at times I would be playing golf . . . other times I was playing an outstanding round, and then all of a sudden, the emotions were overtaking all of me. Also, they even showed women — without any clothes on — as I went through these caverns

— anything they could do to distract me, because they knew I was going to get 'em. The first one I caught was Doubt. Doubt came to me in the figure of a question mark. That's the way Doubt is when you are unsure about what you are going to do at what time. Knowing that I was going to encompass this emotion, and have it within me, rather than around me, I took that question mark in and made it an exclamation point. Then, I put a flag on the end and stuck it in a hole. Now it looks like a golf flag.

I knew at this point that, indeed, I had taken over Doubt because I knew what I wanted and how I was going to get it. As I kept going through the caverns, trying to find the other two emotions, I still had road blocks and hills to climb and valleys to go down into. It seemed to be hard, but as I knew I was coming up on Fear, it stopped. And suddenly, it made the most grotesque face I have ever seen in my entire life . . . just absolutely would scare anybody to death! I grabbed that mist–vapor of green fear around the throat. (For some reason the fear came to me in the color green.) Anyway, I grabbed that bugger around the throat and I looked it right in the eyes. Next, I compressed it. When I compressed it, I made it into a hundred dollar bill. I put it in my back pocket and chugged on. Oh, I knew then without a doubt that they were going to be mine. And Nervousness was *runnin' scared*, I mean he was nowhere to be found. It's like the journey I had to travel was like Dorothy on the Yellow Brick Road. I kept running around the caverns and running, running, running. I came to a castle, with a large green door. I kept beating on the door, trying to get in. Nervousness did not want me to get in. He knew it was his last chance. He could never again control me like he used to on the golf course. I finally got in the door and there stood Nervousness in the form of a large green misty rectangle. Knowing no fear and having no doubt about what I was trying to accomplish, I took that mist in my hands, compressed it into a hundred dollar bill and put it in my back pocket.

"Well," I said to myself as I started back, "you have to encompass them rather than let them encompass you. Nervousness, Fear, and Doubt are always going to be with you, but you have to control them." Now I had two one–hundred dollar bills in my back pocket; one was Nervousness and the other was Fear.

I travelled back through the caverns and the valleys and the mountains — trying to get back somewhere. I just had to get back then. I had them encompassed. As I was travelling back I passed the area where I met and defeated Doubt. My flag was still stuck in the ground. I took the flag out, put it over my shoulder, and started up a long ladder out of the caverns. When I came up through the ground I was on the number one tee at Augusta. Arnold and Jack were waiting for me and they had brought along Ben Hogan to make up the foursome. Arnold and Jack both said the same thing, "Oh, no! Here he comes again!"

Ben Hogan, paying no attention to Arnold and Jack, looked over at me and said, "I don't know who you are, but if you are going to play with me, it's going to cost you two hundred dollars." And I said, "Well, Mr. Hogan, it just so happens that I have two one–hundred dollar bills in my back pocket, and I'll just be glad to give those to you so we can play."

Self–talk or Affirmations?

Self-talk is another type of general image which you can practice until the cows come home and then some. Since your words express thought, they have significant impact on your world. You are aware of your words and will attach your self–image to them. " What a jerk!" you say to yourself as you chunk a sand shot. A strong image, don't you agree?

Your body also finds it strong and will do all it can to comply with the image. That's how good you really are. You're so good that your body will do everything it possibly can to be the image your brain sends down the neuro–pathways. Don't underestimate how efficient your bio–computer is. Program it with verbal software that is to your advantage. You may be saying to yourself that this is too Cinderella–like and that pretending you're something that you don't believe you are is senseless or impractical.

Imagine now that you are standing over the putt you left yourself after chunking the sand shot. Line it up. Stand over it and say to yourself, "I'm such a jerk. Can't even hit a stupid sand shot. Joe really thinks I'm an idiot now. I'm such a fool . . . " and strike your putt. Now line it up again. Stand over it and say to yourself, "I'm a great putter. My breathing relaxes me, and I've created a great image for this shot . . . ." Pause for the deep breath, pause for the image, and strike the putt. Did you feel different physically during each of those two examples? Which putt do you think has the best chance to roll in? Anything you say that is at all tentative can be as destructive as negative comments, so avoid all of the " . . . a" words; i.e., "woulda," "shoulda," "coulda," and "oughta."

Affirmations are images you can introduce to guide your self–talk. They are short phrases like "I'm a great putter" which create a receptive environment in which to image your way around the golf course. When you create them be sure to keep them in the present tense . "I'm a great putter" lets your body know that it is happening now. To say "I will be a great putter in three months" is vague, and your body won't be able to sink its teeth in and internalize the information so that it becomes a reality. Another thing to watch for is the "as soon as I" syndrome. For instance, "I'll be a great putter as soon as I've spent 40 more hours on the practice green." What your body wants to hear is "I am a great putter and I am getting better." Then you can do something with the information. The habituation program of 60 repetitions for 21 consecutive days is an effective image practice format for affirmations. Strong affirmations are very important if you want to develop a general image that gives you clear and vivid images for each shot. These phrases do have their place in the sequence of thoughts that occur as you prepare to play a shot. Your final thought as you strike the ball will be one that is centered around the target, not your self–talk.

Practice Specific Images

Practicing specific images is a powerful technique. You can approach a specific shot or concept in several ways to strengthen your image of it. For example, practice your swing plane in a session. Start with the general relaxation exercise you learned in the Introduction. Guide your brain and body into a rested, relaxed attitude. Find yourself swinging a club. Notice where you are. Change your location on a regular basis. Let the feel and the look of your swing plane sing to you. You may notice the sound of the club swishing through the air. Take on many perspectives. Step outside yourself and watch your swing. Be in front, to each side, stand behind, hover above, look up from underneath, and have the clubface pass over you. Observe the swing plane. Experiment with symbolic images of the plane. Build it out of bricks or let it be in a vacuum between two layers of electrically charged atmospheres that will buzz if the club goes outside the plane's path. See the club swing on its own without you. After you practice with these types and varieties of images, you will know the shape and feel of your swing plane inside–out, backwards and forwards, forever and a day. You can trust your swing plane unequivocally and can take that general image of trust out on the golf course the next time you play.

Think for a moment how well you know what it is to be in a car that makes a right turn. You know that physical experience from the driver's seat, from the back seat, from the street corner observing, at five miles per hour, at 30 miles per hour, in a truck, in a small car, in Missouri, in Oregon. You can recognize it on the television screen — you can image it in several ways. You know what it is to make a right turn. Sometimes the car goes over the curb. Nevertheless, you still know how to execute the right turn. You don't go back to Drivers' Ed. You keep driving and trust your ability to make the next right turn that you take. Your practice of swing plane images reinforces that same quality of trust in what you know.

The Objective Observer

A very important imaging skill for you to develop is that of the objective observer. Create an image of yourself outside of your body. You are there to help, to watch your performance from a different perspective, and to be your own best friend. As the objective observer, you gather information and make discrete calculations that contribute to your game. I have a friend named John Stacy who is so good at this now that he says it feels like "I'm just watching this guy John Stacy live his life."

The more you identify with the objective observer, the more you reduce the build–up of emotionally charged stress and you improve your ability to perceive every stroke. Peter Jacobsen can say, "I didn't miss the putt, the ball missed the hole." You can learn to do the same thing!

Review

This is a good time to review a few things. You have committed to develop the mental mechanics of your game so that you will be able to play more creative, reactive, and fun golf. You will be imaging at home in regular practice sessions; you will be imaging on the range and chipping and putting greens as you reinforce your physical mechanics; you will be imaging on the course as you play. You are thinking all the time. You are imaging all the time. You have realized that fact and are going to tap all that raw material that already bubbles inside you and turn it to your advantage. You are your own support system. You are your own guide. You are both student and teacher for yourself. You are your images. You get what you think. Your golf game is your images of, around, and within it; before, during, and after it. You know this and it makes you feel more confident. Confidence in your abilities is a direct by–product of your image practice. Finally, don't overlook the importance of having fun and being inspired. Cultivate these qualities as you develop images in your golf game. You need a deep sense that "this is a great thing I am doing."

Keep mechanics in their place.

Day 4

Mentally Engaged/ Physically Relaxed

"When playing, success will have been experienced. You have already been there."
Chris Moran, M.D.
1985 S.E.A. Graduate

Here is how to **PLAY** golf:

Go Golf.
Go Create.
Go Re–create (recreate).
Go Liberate, don't deliberate.
Go to the resort and Re–sort.
Make each shot brand new because it is brand new.
Engage with the target, never with the consequences.
Be your own person — your own support system.

Until now there has always been a much greater support system for missing than for making a golf shot. The reason for this is that almost everyone is concerned with the consequences of the shot rather than the content of the shot. The content of the shot is directly controlled by the inner workings of your mind. If you are consequence–oriented, you are in a losing position from the beginning.

"Imagine the ominous pressure of this treacherous little demon of a little downhill slider, ladies and gentlemen. Just imagine how devastating it will be should he let this opportunity slip by him. It could very well destroy his future career."

Such is the commentary coming from the broadcasting booth most Saturdays and Sundays. It is no wonder that the game has become a self–fulfilling prophecy. If you dwell on the outcome or consequences of the shot, then you are in a position of either winning or losing with every shot. Add to this dialectic the belief that the consequence is ominous, devasting, and destroying, and you have instant stress. To maintain the two components of successful performance, play the game with your own images as described by your own vocabulary.

The ingredients for playing up to your personal potential are:

Be mentally engaged with the target
and
Be physically relaxed.

Mental engagement with the target isn't possible when there is an overload or fragmentation of thoughts. If you disregard the consequences of the shot and are completely attached to the images you project about the shot at hand, you are mentally engaged with the target. You have a beginning, middle, and end process for your shot. You will hold this imaged process in your mind for only a few moments during the swing itself. But during that moment the image is precise, vivid, and fully orchestrated. It is the level of engagement with this image that fires the commands from your brain to your body for shot execution. The quality of your shot directly reflects the quality of your images and your engagement with them. A low level of engagement will give vague neuro–muscular commands. A grouping of fragmented images will give vague and confusing neuro–muscular commands. Complete engagement with controlled and precise images will give clear and undisputable neuro–muscular commands. You will achieve your personal potential more frequently when you align yourself with a practice routine and attitude that fosters clear images and high mental engagement.

The second ingredient for maximizing your performance potential is your ability to be in a state of relaxation which will allow your body to react efficiently. If your muscles are tense and tight, the messages your brain sends will not be effective. If your muscles are poised but relaxed, they will function efficiently as the messages are received.

Mentally Engaged

Engage with the Target

You get all of the appropriate instructions from the target. The location, distance, definitions surrounding the target, the wind, elevation, humidity, and all other subtleties are perceived, calculated, and processed by your keen awareness when you are interested in the target. This information is consumed through all of your sensory receivers. Your eyes and ears predominantly sense the information, but smell, feel, and taste can play a part. Your brain processes these sensory images and sends commands to your physical system to respond to the target in direct relationship to the purity and clarity of the incoming information.

This is the same process involved with throwing a ball, hitting a ping pong ball, or driving a car. You take in information through your sensory receivers, process the information with your image–making abilities, and then respond physically through the same sensory devices: visual (sight), kinesthetic (feel), auditory (hearing, vocalization), taste, or smell.

If you are not target–engaged, you are not playing golf! This is the very reason that golfers have a difficult time learning the game. They don't *play* golf. There is a response to some criteria other than the target and its conditions. If you are on the golf course focusing on some portion of your swing, something that you are doing, or an outcome of the shot as it affects you, then you aren't playing golf. Again, this is true in any game. When you shift attention from the target to the outcome (consequence) or to the *how to* of hitting the target, you destroy target orientation.

Keep Your Head Down?

This single most misused phrase in golf instruction is counter–productive. *Keep your head down* is advice intended for a remedy to missing or topping a ball with the clubhead. When you follow this advice, you process images regarding the location of your head during the shot. You are focused on your head rather than on the ball. Isn't it more appropriate to process information on the location of the clubhead relative to the ball rather than focusing your attention on your head?

But most devasting of all is that most golfers are not processing information about the ball relative to the target. The game of golf is made for that single task. To indulge your sensory processes in any task but target intake and response is to be involved with something other than golf. The sad result is twofold.

First, the lack of target awareness never lets you tap the incredible abilities of your mind. Your brain processes information in the neighborhood of 10,000 bits of information per second, about 5000 times faster that you can talk. As you cultivate, practice, and nourish the subtle part of target awareness, you can allow for this amazingly rapid synapse to guide your every action. The end product will be an incredible satisfaction of self liberation. The by–product will be great scores.

Second, there is a growing educational bias that attention to swing, or some part thereof, will make target–oriented shots. In fact, just the opposite is true. You end up processing swing and then judging the end result of the shot instead of the swing. If you are going to process swing, then the *only* proper subject to evaluate is swing. To mix the two is never to evaluate the appropriate subject and make appropriate corrections. At first this may seem very subtle but when you think about it, it is not unlike tasting an orange and saying that it doesn't taste like the apple you wanted.

To *play* golf you need to process the *target*. It doesn't matter if you are a novice or a professional like D. A. Weibring. You will react creatively and proficiently to the target only when you are engaged with the target in the final moments of the swing.

Separate Play from Practice

If you are a novice golfer, I am not suggesting that you will play great golf the first time on the course by purely engaging with the target. If you are an expert, I am saying that you will never play your best golf without engaging with the target. The difference is that the novice and occassional golfer needs to upgrade preswing, swing, and attentional skills off the course. The experienced golfer needs to leave those same skills off the course.

After the beginning golfer habituates grip, stance/posture, routine approach to the ball, and swing concept, there is a period of time needed to refine attentional abilities. Primary is the skill of having the club meet the ball just right in the swing, not too high and not too low. This is accomplished by swinging, then evaluating the relationship of club to ball. If the ball is topped, the club was too high. You must recognize this in your mind's eye. A clear, vivid picture or feeling must be formed so that you can form an equally clear picture or feeling of how the club will meet the ball on the next shot.

This image–making process is the basic foundation to any learning process and the critical foundation of learning golf. It is also a skill that you are easily deprived of by other people telling you how it should be done. They are describing an image that works for them. But, indeed, it is only your focus of attention that counts. Rely on and trust your ingenuity to process information you take in through your senses. Form a strong image in your mind, then respond to the image through your senses.

Continue the process by striking many shots on the driving range, in the backyard of your mind. Be attentive to how your mind processes information. Modify the picture or feeling in your mind. Be quiet and objective as you do so. Isolate what your objective will be for the upcoming task. In a relaxed posture, form the image, execute the image, review the image objectively, and evaluate only its content, and you will know why you got what you got. This is true for both beginners and experts.

The more you practice in this framework, the more elaborate your storehouse of information becomes. Variables which at first seem complicated become routine. The elevation of a shot, the distance of a putt, or the difficulty of a sand shot become an opportunity to modify and create an image for a successful outcome.

Keep Mechanics in Their Place

Whether you are a beginner or an expert, you must keep the mechanics of the game in their place of practice. The truly proper place is the delegation of tasks as defined by your mind. If the task includes a target, it is vital that your image is strictly target–oriented. You may wish to make solid contact between club and ball, a good swing rhythm, a balanced motion, or an extended follow–through. Whatever the task, perform in a relaxed manner and review only the image–making process of that image. On the golf course, the task is the target only.

On the practice tee of Eugene Country Club in July of 1984, Mike Reid demonstrated how effectively his images worked when he applied them to creating specific types of shots. With his driver, he decided that he wanted to hit a low, long–distance drive. The image he used was that the ball was a peach pit and he was going to hit it hard. He smacked the ball and it surged off low and long. Then he decided to hit a high, soft shot with his driver and used an image of the ball as a ripe peach. When his club struck the ball it literally sounded like it had hit a peach. The trajectory was high and the ball landed soft. The difference in the sound of the club head on the ball was as high contrast as night and day. Other people who were practicing and had no idea that Mike and I were working with images stopped to watch. Their attention was captured by the dramatic difference in the sound of the club at impact as Mike switched his trigger image from peach to peach pit. These images took Mike's focus off his body and onto the task at hand, and they were vivid enough that his body complied and performed resoundingly well.

Golf's Scoring Formula

or

How to play better golf by proper delegation of practice

Nearly all golfers, beginner through touring professionals, although having widely divergent scores, have the same shot mix for producing the score.

Using a par 72 full–length course as a model, the mathematics are:

	Pro shoots 72		Amateur shoots 100
Putts	31	43%	43
Short shots (wedges, pitch, chip)	13	18%	18
Full shots	28	39%	39
	72	100%	100

Short shots and putting combine for a whopping 61 percent of your score while full shots represent only 39 percent. So where should your emphasis be? Short game and putting skills can be accomplished at an extremely high performance level by all golfers, regardless of athletic ability. However, you need to practice in the proper area of the scoring formula. The good news is that you can practice in your own backyard or living room. If you recognize the scoring formula and practice accordingly, you will see a significant reduction in your total score.

The Short Game Is Both

Putting, chipping, pitching, and bunker shots are the game in miniature. A single putt on the practice putting green presents the same opportunity for task processing as does the last putt on the last hole of the tournament. You can play the putt with full attention and intention. Gather all the information about the distance, break, and conditions influencing the putt. Narrow that information, and form a crystal clear image of how the putt will start, roll, and fall into the cup. Engage your senses and receive information from the target. Allow the engagement to become more and more vivid until you cannot resist physical action. In the same relaxed posture from which you struck the putt, you should also review the image and evaluate the reason that you got what you got. This scenario is the game of golf.

How to Putt

Step one:　　Aim
Step two:　　Fire
Step three:　　Either get the ball out of the hole or repeat
　　　　　　　　steps one and two.

No joke! Putting is a self–taught discipline based on practice. Practice refines a motor response triggered by target perception or the lack thereof. You either learn to see the putt go in or not go in. In either case, your physical motion corresponds to your image. The proper practice techniques, both physical and mental, performed in a routine and disciplined manner are the only remedies for overcoming a deficiency in effective target orientation.

The Best Time to Practice

It is so easy to alibi and avoid playing well and having fun by saying that you don't have the time to play enough golf. But if you look carefully, you'll see that you can enjoy the ease and convenience of practicing in your living room, backyard, or at the golf course putting and chipping green. You can put full attention and intention into each practice shot. Better yet, call the practice shot the real thing. *Do not* put consequence into the shot but do become fully engaged and relaxed physically. Fill in all the details to the shot and play it to its fullest.

Here are some image exercises to help you develop your short game mentally. Read through them first so that you won't need to refer to the book while you are imaging, and then turn your attention to one or more of these topics during an image session. Begin with the general relaxation exercise in the Introduction.

1. Recall the concept of ball spin characteristics that you use in tennis, ping–pong, etc. Relate the swing plane involved with each of these strokes.
2. Cross reference a cut–shot of a pitch shot with that of a ping– pong shot. See the ball spin of each shot. See and feel the beginning, middle, and end of each of these shots. Notice how your hand feels the ball on the paddle/clubface. There is a relatively high left–to–right trajectory. Watch the ball land softly and stop very quickly. Notice the end result on the green.
3. Follow the same procedure with chipping. Notice the entire shot in your mind's eye, particularly the end result.
4. Putting is nearly the same as chipping. In both cases, the end result is of ultimate importance. The ball must stop at the exact range you choose, so the feel of how much energy you use must be precise. Make sure that each imaged shot has a well–defined destination. Roll the ball over the front lip of the hole or slam it in the back. However you choose to make the shot, do so with total perfection in depth (distance). Practice the involvement of as many senses as possible to help elaborate and complete your see/feel picture. Can you smell the dirt in the hole? What does the grass under–foot feel like? What color is the sky?

Are You Practicing to Miss?

When Dale Van Dalsem and I were at Winged Foot for the 1984 U.S. Open, we happened to be standing near the putting green, watching the contestants practice. Dale turned to me and asked "Why are all the guys practicing missing?"

It was profoundly true. The best golfers in the world were practicing missing. They would either give haphazard effort to the target and then reprimand themselves as the ball missed, or they would obviously be working on a mechanical stroke, giving only lip service to target and then miss and reprimand themselves.

There is only one thing worse than hitting a bad shot and not knowing why. That one thing is to hit a good shot and not know why! This statement is validated by the way the Open players were practicing. It is also validated by any practice procedure that does not put intention, relaxation, and review into every shot. Again, the content of your thought (images) must be the review, not the consequences of the shot.

You can use the short shots of golf for any task. You can habituate preswing functions. You can imprint conceptual understanding of club function, or you can experiment with and play with creating shots with appropriate reactions to the target and its conditions. You must select only one of the tasks to preview, perform, and review. This requires attention and discipline, but so does the shot on the course. The shot on the course must be oriented to target processing, and you can practice this skill as effectively in your backyard as you can on number 18 at Pebble Beach.

Peter Jacobsen often practices putting without a ball. There he is, on the putting green enacting the complete procedure without a ball. He reads it, gets over the non–existent ball, and knocks it in. To Peter, the entire shot is processed to perfection. His subconscious mind does not discriminate between the real ball and the imagined ball. His muscles and bones do not discriminate. So if Peter is always successful with the processing of the task, won't it reflect in more success more of the time?

Muscle Memory Doesn't Exist!

Most avid golfers hit thousands of balls and practice hundreds of hours under the assumption that they are storing memory into their muscles. The fact is that muscles do not have the capacity to store information. Hitting balls is important for toning and strengthening muscles, but storage is a brain function.

Information storage is an extremely important piece of the confidence formula, so store the most appropriate information. As you prepare for a practice shot you will want to preview success. Each repetition fires a signal through your brain and files it into a storage bin. As you clarify and intensify the contact, flight and end result of the shot repeatedly fire more signals to the storehouse. As you review the shot, evaluate the image process, and modify its content for future success, you are storing more signals.

It is easy to see that you can be storing both more signals and more appropriate signals by discriminating practice than by indiscriminate practice. When you accept the appropriate concept of this storage process, it means then that you also have to accept responsibility for your own practice habits. If you practice by hitting thousands of balls in a random manner, half paying attention to what you are doing, and then degrade yourself for poor shots, what are you storing? On the other hand, imagine the rewards of attentive practice which gives careful reinforcement to appropriate thoughts and is non-emotional regarding inappropriate images.

The concept of *overlearned skills* also falls into the area of message storage. By far the quickest and most enduring storage of any behavior is to put in exactly the proper criteria. If you want to draw upon successful experiences, you must store successful experiences. The old cliché of *garbage in–garbage out* is most appropriate. But the good news is also *success in–success out*! Which do you want?

You Are on Your Own

One most notable feature of this book is the absence of telling you how to play golf. There is no advice as to what club to use, how far to hit the ball, or the technique of hitting a shot higher than normal. I believe that your habituation of pre–swing skills, your total conceptualization of golf club design, and your imagination and powers of observation are not only all you need but the only way to ultimately enjoy and become proficient at the game.

Golf is a game **to** play and it is also a game **of** play. Play with your images as they relate to the target. Take in all the information from books, magazines, good players, and every resource available to you. Weigh this information in light of preswing fundamentals and the concept of club design. You will quickly discard 95 percent of incoming advice as a quick fix or inaccurate information. You will watch the skills of good golfers and understand why their club is doing what it does. Interpet these observations, synthesize and reform the image to fit the individual person you are.

It is not only okay to be on your own but it is the essence of the game. Play with the notion of improvement not as a goal but as an ongoing process. Or, as the old saying says, "Live and Learn."

Learning to strike a putt with exact energy to roll the ball the exact distance is a classic example of self–learning. There are some very strange and equally silly pieces of advice to tell you how to hit the ball. In truth, only experience can teach you the proper energy to throw, kick, or hit a ball a chosen distance. Your perception of the target provokes a calculation. This calculation is an image transferred to action through kinesthetic sensory processes. The evaluation of the outcome forms another image of the ball traveling too far, too short, or just right. Repeating this experience and the image–making process is how your system learns the proper response to the given conditions. This is the creative process. This is the game to be relished.

You Get What You Think

Thinking is the image processing experience. Words are the description of the experience, not the experience itself. This is why you must evaluate the content of the image itself through a non–judgmental vocabulary to understand that you get what you think.

For example, if you think of water hazard as you initiate your backswing and the ball splashes into the middle of the water, have you shot a bad shot? Actually, it is a perfect shot. The efficiency of the process is incredibly wonderful. Your brain imaged water. Your body got the message and performed in relationship to the purity, vividness, and orchestration of your image. Splash!

One of our clients held an idea (image) of making the cut of each tournament. The dominant thought was to make the cut and therefore be able to play on Saturday and Sunday. During the first half of 1985, he had a total of 84 strokes over par after Thursday and Friday's round. He had the sum figure of three strokes over par for the total of Saturday and Sunday rounds. This is the same player with same *physical* skills. The only difference was his attitude (image) toward performance. His body carried out the image with perfect efficiency. With his image of making the cut, his body achieved the cut. Once that was accomplished, he felt he could relax and just play. His body responded by putting the ball into the hole with significantly fewer strokes.

You must be clear on this point: *you will get what you think.* What you think is the intake of information (stimulus), the processing of information, and the output of information. This is the imaging process. Words are not the process, only a weak description. You have the choice to think what you want and determine the outcome of your activity.

Be Perceptually Flexible

All great athletes are abnormal. If they were normal they wouldn't be great. One major difference between good golfers and great golfers is the ability to take a different view of a situation. Where one person sees trouble and forms an image of failure, another sees opportunity for creating success. When some players hit the ball into the trees, they may be thinking bogey or double bogey. Tom Watson, most likely, is thinking birdie or par. Not only does Tom perform up to this attitude and expectation, but his opponent is crushed by his coming through the rough unscathed.

It is vital that you do not believe in the commonly accepted expectations of the golf community. Pressure on a putt exists only to the degree that you give it attention. Nothing more, nothing less. You have to ask yourself if the belief in pressure is to your advantage or disadvantage.

Golf vernacular is full of phrases and clichés that form belief systems, perceptions, and attitudes that affect performance. Become an astute observer of these idioms. Disregard the inappropriate ones and nurture those which are fitting to a healthy attitude and frame of mind. Your ability to discriminate the incoming impressions does not mean that you are arrogant or stand–offish. Play the game of choosing what you want. Be flexible in how you perceive information. Learn to view and approach every situation and every comment so that it is to your advantage.

Ben Hogan has reportedly stated that he played his entire career with a cultural belief system that did not work to his advantage. Conventional golfing wisdom states that you should play the ball into the green so that the ball is positioned below the hole, leaving a reasonably makeable putt. Ben Hogan now believes he should have been playing the shot into the green and into the hole! Why leave any putt? Let me reinforce this idea by saying that the hole is only there for the purpose of receiving the ball!

Surrender to the Target

The final and most elusive skill of creativity on the golf course is the ability to truly receive and react to the information that the target has for you. It is a process of merging with the target so that the target hits you more than you hit it. It is within the slow brain wave potential of deeply felt images accompanied with a poised relaxation that this occurs. You blend with the demands of the task, not blocking or censoring any outside or inside information. You take in everything and synthesize the information to deliver the most accurate commands to your muscles.

All of this happens rapidly and silently, absent of internal or external dialogue. Any concern for consequences of the outcome or swing mechanics gives way to total engagement with your target and the ball arriving at the target. Along with this end result, the process of the shot is clear to you. You see and feel the shape and the beginning of the shot that are necessary to produce the end result. This target–stimulated focus clearly directs the messages that your body receives as it expects the shot. Any shift in awareness to self will disassociate you from the target and its information. When the shot is completed, you might very well shift your attention back to yourself in the surprise of how successful and easy the experience was. A better response is to review the actuality that your target engagement was rich and that the flight and beginning of your shot were clear and lined up with the target before and during your swing. You created appropriate software and got an advantageous printout. You created and stayed engaged with a vivid target–oriented image. You were very much *in* your mind. It is unfortunate that golf language describes this supreme quality of performance as *out of my mind* or *on a roll*. After each shot, review the clarity and content of your target–oriented image. Take credit where credit is due and make improvement where improvement is due. Strive to hit each shot with all your lights on, and don't be fooled when your playing partners describe your performance as "Wow, you just played *lights out* today." Jack Nicklaus has often been quoted as saying that he "willed the ball into the hole." He isn't kidding about this; he is clearly imaging it.

Physically Relaxed

If you absolutely had to choose between developing one or the other of the two performance ingredients, mentally engaged or physically relaxed, I would prefer that you choose to spend time increasing your relaxation skills. My reason is that you need to be sensitive and flexible physically if you are going to be able to respond to your images. Also, a state of poised physical relaxation is necessary for you to create really clear images and respond mentally to the target. Finally, I am certain that a well–developed skill in relaxation alone will raise your enjoyment of the game and help you improve your score.

Michelangelo may have had tremendous inspiration for what to paint on the Sistine Chapel ceiling, but we would not be able to enjoy that work today if he hadn't had the physical poise to let the brush flow in his hand. Had his arm been too tense, he would not have been able to execute his vision regardless of its clarity or his proficiency as a painter. Your state of ease on the golf course is what enables you to respond with the physical skills you have to the images you have.

This has been demonstrated to me frequently. One recent example is a client who participated in an S.E.A. Golfing Excellence school this summer in St. Louis. Jim Robertson is an avid golfer. He is 40 years old, an 18 handicapper, and starting on his third summer of golf. He played basketball into his 30s and has kept up an active exercise program throughout his adult life. He approached me on the driving range after playing nine holes and was perplexed about his drives. At that point, he was into the 17th day of a swing plane habituation program and felt very encouraged by his image engagement on the practice tee. During the 21–day period, Jim also played golf several times and felt he was successful in creating and engaging in target–oriented images. For the last few rounds he had played, he noticed that his drives started off great and travelled to his target accurately and with a trajectory that resulted from an inside–out swing plane. Along about the fourth hole, however, he felt he was staying mentally engaged with his target–oriented images, and yet the ball's trajectory indicated that he was executing an outside–in swing plane which did not deliver the ball to the target. We tossed out the possible impediments to his success at aligning his physical action with the target image. I suggested he could simply be getting tired physically, or that his image was breaking down somewhere. He felt certain that he wasn't tiring because he was doing an exercise and running program that made him feel stronger than he had in years. It was possible that either the beginning, middle, or end of his image was vague or perhaps he was shifting from target awareness to self–awareness. He also felt that his enthusiasm for the imagery was intense, that his mental engagement with the target was high, that his images were indeed complete, and that he was not shifting from target to swing plane images on the course.

Puzzled, he went off with his driver and began a sorting-through process. A half–hour later he reappeared to tell me that he had noticed tension in his shoulders that started with his grip and forearms as he addressed the ball. This prevented him from getting a shoulder turn that could allow him to send the ball to his chosen target. He then decided to develop an image of relaxation to put into his preshot routine that dissolved the symptom and began to make inside–out swings that responded to his target image.

Three things impressed me about this interaction. First, Jim was certain that his target image orientation was fine. He did not automatically conclude that he was projecting incomplete images. I have witnessed many people make the latter choice without batting an eyelash or putting up a fight as they decide that the whole *imaging thing* is far too difficult. They assume the motto " You can't teach an old dog new tricks" and then promptly set about finding some mechanical flaw that they need to dissect. The second thing that impressed me was that his decision that he was projecting target and not swing plane images on the course was really based on his intuition. He had the ability to stick with his intuition in a time when rationality and focus on symptoms could easily have aborted it. The third thing was that he had the sensitivity to recognize that tension in his shoulders.

Another non–golf scenario that I have seen several times is the pass receiver at a football game who is wide and clear, has his arms outstretched, and the ball just bounces off of his hands as if they were concrete. This phenomenon could be the result of either lack of mental engagement or physical relaxation, but often it appears to me that his hands were simply too tense to grasp and hold onto the ball. He may have that pass pattern down cold and be able to perform it in his sleep, but if his hands are inflexible at the moment the play happens during a game, all that practice is for naught.

You need to develop the skills that help you relax, but you don't want to be so relaxed that you become a blasé blob of jello. Actually, a level of stress is healthy for you. The medical field calls this level eustress. "Eu–" is a prefix that indicates well being. Your eustress level is necessary for you to roll out of bed in the morning and have the wherewithall to navigate your car down the road. With regular physical relaxation practice, you can learn to recognize when your eustress level is about to go over the line into stress. You will recognize what parts of your body manifest the first signs that stress has arrived to override eustress. You also have the benefit of relieving daily build–up of stress as you practice relaxation regularly.

The distinction between stress and eustress is similar to another very important distinction, which is the difference between being serious and being intense. When you are serious about your golf game you are placing your attention on yourself rather than on the target. When you are intense about golf, you are placing your attention on the target and the target objective. Watch a three–year–old child with building blocks. She's over in the corner creating a world, very intent on the activity, with no thought of herself. That *is* the world and reality as far as she is concerned. She is imaging, creating, and that is the same quality of intensity that you can bring to the golf course. Whatever you do, don't be serious. If you find that you are, then use it as an opportunity to redirect your attention. Deep breathing techniques are one very quick and efficient way to lead you from seriousness to intensity and from stress to eustress. They can be used on the course between shots as a matter of habit to keep your mind clear and steer it away from becoming fragmented and unfocused.

All peak performance is characterized by varying degrees of increased slow brain wave activity. Faster brain waves, categorized as beta, are capable of processing and carrying several bits of unrelated information at any one time. Conversations and self–talk fall into the beta frequency, and during your waking hours your brain waves are predominately in beta. Unlike the faster beta waves, the alpha and theta states, characterized by slower brain wave frequencies, reflect a harmonization and thematic image unity. There is still plenty of information being processed with your slowed wave frequencies. Rather than looking like backed–up air traffic at Kennedy International Airport, they look like the concentric circles created when you toss a pebble into a pond. This serenity is deceiving and is often referred to as *no mind.* In fact, it is all mind. You process enormous quantities of information and are able to respond to a single topic (i.e., your target) with a thorough understanding of the conditions you are operating in.

Since talk and verbalization are members of the beta group, slowed brain waves are also characterized as being non–verbal yet extremely rich in images. Most of your dreams are created within theta and alpha brain wave frequencies, and when you are in deep sleep without dreams your waves are even slower. This state is called delta. You will not play much golf with the delta wave frequencies, but you will be playing more and more golf within the alpha and theta frequencies as you learn to be more mentally engaged and physically relaxed. Your commitment to use deep breathing, to develop a close awareness of your states of eustress and stress, and to notice where tension tends to locate in your body means that you will have the ability to guide yourself into slowed brain wave frequencies easily.

The following exercises are a system of self–guided relaxation called autogenics developed in the 1930's by Dr. Johannes Schultz. The system is easy to learn and requires only consistent practice and imagination splashed with affirmations to achieve the goal of controlling physiological functions such as heart rate, blood pressure, and body temperature. I have outlined the program here and have modified it to fit into 21–day segments. Use the habit formation chart on page 30 to chart your progress.

This system is used extensively in the Eastern block countries and is credited with putting athletes on the cutting edge that separates the great from the good, the frequent peak performance from the accidental peak performance, and the winners from the also–rans. Take yourself through this program. You will find that the benefits you derive are well worth the 7–15 minutes you devote to practice. Remember that it doesn't matter how vivid, detailed, and controlled your images are unless your body is capable of responding to them. Take one 21–day sequence at a time. Be careful to begin a sequence at a time when your schedule won't be interrupted by things like travel, visitors, or a heavier work load. These activities in themselves won't keep you from practicing, but you may think that they affect your discipline. If you can, continue to schedule time during unusual breaks in your daily routine.

Autogenics Practice

Lie down or sit in a comfortable position and start with the general relaxation exercise from the Introduction. Begin by synchronizing your breath with your heartbeats. Find your pulse.

> Inhale through your nose over the count of six beats.
> Hold your breath for three beats.
> Exhale through your mouth for six beats.
> Hold for three beats.
> Begin the cycle again.

Once you feel your breathing has made you relaxed, your next step is to put on a relaxation mask. Imagine that your scalp, ears, forehead, eyes, cheeks, jaw, mouth, chin, and neck are relaxed. Let the tension wash away from your face. Create an image or several images of this mask. Always start each session with relaxation that includes deep breaths and follow it with a relaxation mask. When your mask is in place, begin the actual exercise.

The exercises entail repeating phrases to yourself. It is beneficial to do these repetitions as you exhale rather than as you inhale. This is not a necessity but you may find it creates an effective rhythm.

Six 21–Day Programs

1. Heaviness

	Repetitions
My _____ is getting limp and heavy	6-8
My _____ is getting heavier and heavier	6-8
My _____ is completely heavy	6-8
I feel supremely calm	1

Repeat this series 3 times per session. Each time you begin a series shake out your limbs or stretch. Be sure your relaxation mask is on. Put it back on if you notice that it is gone or ineffective. Start with your right arm and work with it for 3 days. If you're left–handed, start with your left arm. Here is a list of the order and number of days to do each limb or pair of limbs.

Order	Days
Right arm	3
Left arm	3
Both arms	3
Right leg	3
Left leg	3
Both legs	3
Both arms and legs	3
TOTAL	21

As you repeat these phrases, back up the words with several types of images. Your body understands images. Repeat the phrases with total attention and intention. Fill your message at the sub–talk level with images. For instance, when you say the words *limp* and *heavy,* you can form images of warm, wet noodles for limp, and a solid steel suitcase for heavy. Find several images for these sensations. They will be the most efficient guides for your body.

2. Warmth

Begin with one complete cycle of heaviness for both arms and legs together so that you are feeling heavy before you begin to work on warmth.

My arms and legs are getting limp, heavy and warm	6-8
My arms and legs are getting heavier and heavier	6-8
My arms and legs are completely heavy	6-8
I feel supremely calm	1

Then use the same order and repetitions as you did in the above program. Change the phrases to this:

	Repetitions
My _____ is getting limp, heavy and warm	6-8
My _____ is getting warmer and warmer	6-8
My _____ is completely warm	6-8
I feel supremely calm	1

Repeat this series three times per session. Remember to check your relaxation mask, be sure that your breathing is calm and well paced, and to create images of warmth to accompany the words you are saying.

3. Heartbeat

Begin with a full cycle of "My arms and legs are getting limp, heavy, and warm; are getting heavier and warmer; are completely heavy and warm; I feel supremely calm." When you feel heavy and warm repeat these phrases:

	Repetitions
My chest feels warm and pleasant	6-8
My heartbeat is calm and steady	6-8
I feel supremely calm	6-8

Repeat this series three times per session for 21 days. Remember your deep breathing, relaxation mask, and images.

4. Breathing

	Repetitions
My arms and legs are getting limp, heavy, and warm	2
My arms and legs are getting heavier and warmer	2
My arms and legs are completely warm	2
My heartbeat is calm and steady	2
I feel supremely calm	2
My breathing is supremely calm	8
It breathes me	1

Repeat this series three times per session for 21 days. Let your breathing, relaxation mask, and images guide you in this process.

5. Stomach

Use the breathing series above and modify only the number of repetitions of "My breathing is supremely calm." Change them from 8 repetitions to 2 and after the phrase "It breathes me," add:

	Repetitions
My stomach is getting soft and warm	8
I feel supremely calm	1

Repeat this series three times per session. Remember to support your words with images and to check your relaxation mask before beginning the next series.

6. Forehead

Repeat the above series, reducing the phrase "My stomach is getting soft and warm" to two repetitions. Then add:

	Repetitions
My forehead is cool	8
I feel supremely calm	1

Repeat this series three times per session. Remember your mask, breathing, and images.

Final formula for autogenics

	Repetitions
My arms and legs are heavy and warm	1
My heartbeat and breathing are calm and steady	1
My stomach is soft and warm, my forehead is cool	1
I feel supremely calm	1

Precede the formula with some deep breaths and your relaxation mask, and you will be able to use it to relax you as you wait for the foursome ahead of you that is holding up play, or to offset any situation you think may create tension for you.

As you practice this on a daily basis, finish each session with an affirmation. You will be relaxed and receptive and it is a perfect time for a message to sink in. Phrases like "I'm a great putter" or "I have boundless energy" are examples of appropriate thoughts to affirm at this rich time. Use images to fill out the phrases and make them more real.

There are several other ways to enhance your state of physical well–being. Regular exercise makes a significant contribution. Stress and tension are reduced as you work out to keep your muscles flexible and toned and as you strenghten your heart and lungs. Also, try to avoid the stress caused by playing golf. Because the golf swing motion is one–sided, most professional golfers have back problems during their careers. You can guard against this source of stress with exercises that are simple and address the golf muscle groups specifically. (See Appendix B. Along with exercise, make it a point to take saunas, steams, and hot tubs, and schedule in regular massages on at least a monthly basis.)

Images are M.E. (Mentally Engaged)

In the S.E.A. golf schools, the imagery sessions are conducted with the use of sounds generated by the Mindshapes III Image Generator created by Dale Van Dalsem. The machine generates pure electronic tones which, when listened to on stereo headsets, create an environment of sound that stimulates a frequency following response in the listener's brain. The result is a shift into a greater predominance of slow wave frequencies and the clients are able to experience profound physical relaxation and extremely vivid imagery in a very short while. The tones are unusual, stimulating, and they make it easy for you to identify readily with the states of mental engagement and physical relaxation that are characteristic of peak performance. I have seen that listening to the tones makes a dramatic difference in the quality of accomplishment during the initial stages of mental imagery practice, and that they are also beneficial to use on a maintenance basis once regular practice is begun. Tapes of these tones are available in record and book stores throughout the country and their titles are *Mindshapes, Images are M.E.*, and *Inside–Out*. You may also order them direct from the publisher with the form provided at the back of this book.

The tones, breathing, autogenics skills, exercise, and physically relaxing activities like massages are ways to foster confidence. If you walk onto the golf course relaxed and poised, aware that you have skills to monitor your state of physical relaxation during the time you are out there playing, you will have brought with you some key components of confidence to contribute to your ability to stay mentally engaged and create golf shots with vivid and controlled images.

Day 5

Reinforce the Triangle Walls

"The way to be comfortable in a state of grace is to practice being comfortable in a state of grace."
Jim Robertson
Sales Trainer and Author
1985 S.E.A. Graduate

This chapter will show you how to develop a network of support skills that let you play all of your golf game. You are assuming a lot more responsibility for the game you play by practicing and trusting your images. You are gathering information and shaping your response to that information. You can have your cake and eat it too. There's just more to the cake than meets the eye. I know that my words can only describe the cake. I can talk until I'm blue in the face, and it won't hold a candle to what you experience when the fork actually makes it into your mouth. My words can only describe the experience; they are not the experience. It is important that you accept things on your own and that you believe them because of your own experience, not because someone else has told you it should be one way or the other.

This is your first piece of cake: Your words, self–talk, and affirmations are not your golf shot. They can describe the shot. They can ready your frame of mind to create the shot. But the buck stops here. The golf shot is the image you have just as you take the club back and as it goes through. It is the images below the surface of talk that carry the current to your muscles and trigger your physical motion. There is literally no time elapsed between what you image and what you do. They are actually one and the same thing.

The Upside–Down Triangle

The image of an upside–down triangle is the clearest example I have found for representing all the types of images and their appropriate positioning in the shot–making process. The image of going out on the course and gritting your teeth for four hours in serious concentration is an image from the past, and that's exactly where it should stay. It portrays an ineffective way to concentrate. It's golfing with blinders on. The amount of energy you consume when you play this way will beat anyone to pieces. Another portrayal is concentration that flows from a general to specific or broad to narrow focus. How else do you get to smell the roses and make putts during the same round? How else do you get to be physically relaxed and mentally engaged for four hours. If you shoot 85 strokes for 18 holes, you only need to be there for 170 seconds and that is if your swing takes two seconds. If you shoot 65, it takes only 130 seconds. Most golf swings take considerably less time than that. It is only during the swing that the rheostat needs to be at 100 percent wattage. The rest of the time you can conserve your energy. The remaining 3 hours, 57 minutes, and 10 seconds of your round you can be in a broad focus mode. Each stroke occurs at the bottom point of the triangle. All your calculations, self–talk, club selection, and alignment decisions are made in the upper two–thirds of the triangle.

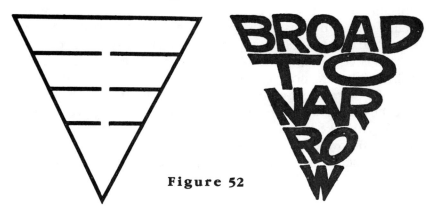

Figure 52

The Triangle of Shot Efficiency, or Think Broad to Narrow

If you were to graph the golf shot information process, the graph would look like an upside down triangle. Your cognitive processes should be in a very wide information gathering mode as you prepare for the shot and narrow to a very isolated thought (image) at the moment of impact. When your mind is operating in this effective state, the messages being delivered through your nervous system are very articulate. The muscles and tendons responsible for the motor actions of your swing are given precise information and have no choice but to follow the instructions (provided, of course, that the physical tone of the muscles is intact). You have undoubtedly experienced the excellent shot that results from this thinking process. Now you can learn to manage the triangle to keep the shots coming.

General Target Orientation

The first step is to consume as much information as possible regarding any factor affecting the shot. Quietly consume the distance to the hole, the lie of the ball, the shape and contours of the fairway, green and bunkers, the wind, topography, club selection, and anything else that influences your shot. This is not just an analytical act but also an intuitive process. It may take a very few seconds to a minute or two, depending upon the conditions and your frame of mind at the time. Nevertheless, you want to be fully receptive to the demands of the shot, and you do that with a very broad focus of attention. The orientation of target is general.

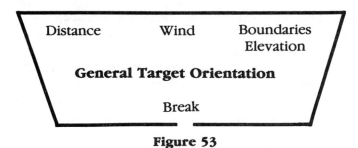

Figure 53

Routine Approach To The Ball

The second portion of information processing is more specific. You are now in your routine approach to the ball, and the thoughts surrounding the settling into the shot are turned inward. You are concerned with aiming your body and the clubface. You have a sense of balance and readiness for an accurate shot. This period of time may be five to twenty seconds for very methodical preparers like Jack Nicklaus or you may be very quick like Lee Trevino. Regardless of the time element, your thoughts must be fewer and more refined than in the first part of the triangle.

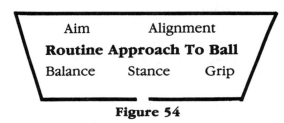

> Aim   Alignment
> **Routine Approach To Ball**
> Balance   Stance   Grip

Figure 54

Traditionally, the golfers of the world are in a common approach in the first third of the triangle. It is the approach in the last two–thirds which often distinguishes the fifteen handicapper from the five handicapper, the good putter from the yipper, or the winning professional from the 25th finish. The bottom of the triangle must continue to narrow as your thoughts become more specific for efficient neuro–processing.

Target Specifics

The next portion of thought is limited to specific target orientation. During this phase, you very clearly image the flight (trajectory and curve), landing, bounce, roll, and destination of the ball. The same considerations also apply to pitch, chip, or sand shots. Putting also is fully developed in pre–swing or feeling the line, speed, and successful holing of the putt. Being fully engaged in the specific target orientation you have, by definition, leaves no room for outside, mechanical, or superfluous thoughts. Your neuro–system is receiving the most direct commands for successful shot completion. The time involved in this awareness may be less than a second to a few seconds.

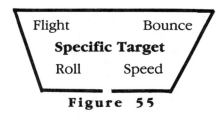

Figure 55

You will notice that there is a passageway or attachment from the third to the last portion of thinking. The bottom of the triangle is reserved for a predetermined single and precise thought or sensation, i.e., an image. This trigger image is held through the swing motion and during contact. This final thought mixes with and facilitates the specific target engagement but is held primary in your mind. The time involved is certainly less than a second (usually just the duration of the forward swing to impact). Use any image you find most appropriate and engaging.

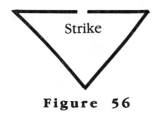

Figure 56

The Total Picture

Intellectually, you may initially find this approach to be complicated, manufactured or mechanical. In retrospect, however, you can look back on great rounds and great shots and find that you were employing this triangle of thought effectively. You can also cross reference to other games and sports and find that cognitive activity follows the same form. Focus goes from wide to narrow, with the reactive sequence of events triggered by the narrowing of thought focus at the bottom of the triangle. Consistent practice of broad to narrow focusing develops into a learned and repeatable skill, and it eventually begins to feel quite natural.

The total picture of the efficient process looks like this:

Figure 57

Inefficient and fragmented thinking will make the bottom of the triangle fall apart. If you allow yourself to fall into the common notion of swing mechanics, you will actually expand and disrupt nerve paths with an overload of information. Your body's motor responses will be confused and disarranged with the input of divergent bio–chemical commands. The triangle and the shot appear something like this:

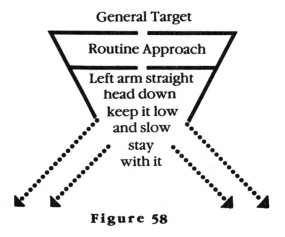

Figure 58

To avoid the interference of excessive thoughts, you need:

1) objective reflection after each shot to evaluate your broad to narrow thinking,

2) a freshness to the final image which keeps you mentally engaged,

3) the physical relaxation necessary for precise motor response,

4) the commitment to keep mechanics on the practice tee, and

5) the discipline always to view the target as a primary activator for your swing.

In between shots you are very broad and relaxed. You have already determined how complete your previous image was, and you are free to put your mind totally into walking down the course. This is a good time to joke around, have fun, and take deep breaths. As you travel around the course your round looks like this:

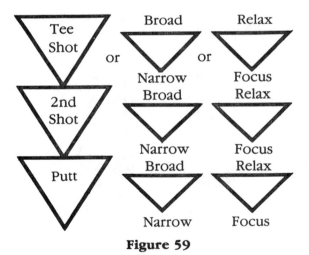

Figure 59

Daily practice of imagery will really help you strengthen the walls of your triangle. Intrusive thoughts will not enter your mind. You will trust yourself more and develop the ability to control your images as well as make them vivid and fresh. The control is very important because it can be easy to get distracted and fragmented. Your level of physical relaxation and commitment to your images feeds into your ability to select and engage with images that will get the ball to the hole in the fewest number of strokes. Without control, relaxation, and commitment, you will take more strokes.

Use the image of the two thermometers in figure 60 on the golf course. Ten is the highest level of mental engagement and physical relaxation that you can achieve. Ask yourself frequently where these levels are, specifically before and after you make a shot. This will help you stay relaxed, receptive, and objective.

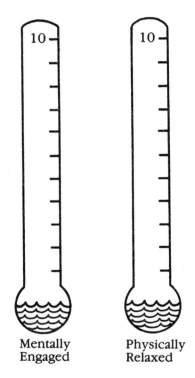

Figure 60

Other Factors That Affect Your Game

Physical exercise on a regular basis keeps your body flexible and toned and allows it to respond to the images and signals that you send it. Take into account what your physical condition is when you review your image and how clear it is. A vivid image of a 250–yard tee shot may fall short in actuality when the image is created by a five–year–old girl wielding her daddy's driver. Physical conditioning supports your images. For instance, if you are practicing images of increased clubhead velocity, it is appropriate to begin a program to strengthen your muscles. Most golfers do not exercise their posterior muscles as much as their frontal muscles. This imbalance contributes to an outside–in violation during the forward swing. In Appendix B I have included a series of exercises which specifically apply to golf muscle groups. This is a simple program that will strengthen your posterior muscles and support your inside–outside swing motion. If you are not already on a program, these exercises are a good basic starting point. They do not in any way replace the benefits you can gain from a program designed for you specifically by an exercise physiologist. Be kind to yourself. If you don't have the desire or don't choose to make the time for physical exercise, then don't expect to be able to perform like a super athlete on the golf course.

Nutritional Recommendations

The food you eat provides the energy that your muscles use to strike the golf ball. There has been considerable research showing that complex carbohydrates provide the most easily accessible energy to your muscles. Here are some general recommendations:

Eat more complex carbohydrates. You can get complex carbohydrates from these foods: brown rice, pasta, whole grain breads and cereals, potatoes, beans, peas, most fresh fruits and vegetables.

Eat less animal protein, particularly red meat.

Reduce your fat intake, particularly saturated fats.

Eat less simple carbohydrates (sugar, for instance).

Drink at least eight glasses of water every day.

Golf demands the mental concentration and focus of a surgeon, as well as exquisite and elegant neuromuscular coordination. Under the stress of competition your blood sugar can plummet to hypoglycemic levels. It is a good idea to carry a readily available source of complex carbohydrates, such as apples, bananas, dried fruit or whole wheat bagels to snack on. It is also a good idea to carry water or diluted fruit juice (2 tbsp. juice to 1 cup of water, with a little salt) and drink some at every tee. Thirst is not a good indicator of your need for fluids, so drink before you are thirsty.

If the topic of nutrition sparks your interest, consult a nutritionist who will determine a program suited for your own metabolism and activities. Your diet, just like your physical conditioning, contributes to your ability to construct triangles that will not break down.

Prepare Yourself Mentally

Prepare yourself mentally before each round you play. Make the time to relax, do some deep breathing, and image your way around the course before you go. If it is a course you've never played, build an overall image that includes swing plane, tempo, and feel. When you make the time to hit some shots on the driving range before a round, start by warming up physically with some head rolls and stretching. Warm your images up as well as your body. Hit a few balls until you have a clear feeling of connection between your images, your body, and the club. During and after the round, review each shot on the basis of the clarity, vividness, and appropriateness of the image that preceded each shot. Take notes during this review and use them to help you choose how you can best spend your practice time both on the range and in image sessions off the course.

When you are competing, add an activity which will really familiarize you with the course you are to play. If at all possible, make the time to walk the course either early in the morning or late in the afternoon. The shadows on the course at these times will display the contours that it has to offer you when you play. Walk backwards starting on the 18th green. Get to know the course as a friend without your clubs. You may be astounded at how wide the fairways are and how the *trouble spots* take on the role of definition rather than trouble. Walk along the out-of-bounds boundaries and familiarize yourself with the territory. A relaxed walk like this can prepare you for a *walk in the park* during competition.

A very important imaging activity as you prepare for competition is to preview winning. Explore how it feels and what the implications are. You want to go into a round with the confidence that you will not be distracted when you build each triangle for each shot. Is it pressure to win? Do you need to prepare a speech? Recognize that these considerations can fragment your triangles unless you take care of them before you tee it up. Symbolic images can contribute greatly to your effectiveness in coming to terms with issues such as pressure or deserving to win. Here is an example of an image session that one client had regarding his perception of pressure.

Wednesday Afternoon Sound Session

Larry Aspenson is an assistant golf pro at Waverly Country Club in Portland, Oregon. This is what happened for him on his third day of the S.E.A. Sunriver Golf School held in October of 1984. Larry is an extremely soft-spoken young man, a man of few words. However, when he uses the MS III Image generator tones for his image sessions, he unravels miles of vivid images all strung together in a marvelous story-telling style. Here is Larry's story:

> I began the session with the usual procedure, getting comfortable and doing some deep breathing. I followed the suggestion of counting backwards from ten to zero picturing each number illuminating the blackness of my mind. At the bottom of the stairs was a large green metal door. On the door was a sign similar to warning signs found on high voltage transformers. It read DANGER: HIGH PRESSURE in bold black letters on a white background with black trim. Next to the words on each side was a black lightning bolt.
>
> I put my hand on the door knob. At first it felt very hot; the next instant it was very cold. As I

opened the door, the door knob kept feeling hot, then cold. I went inside and found myself in an old hotel lobby. A reddish mist filled the air. The room was hot and smelled like sulphur or rotten eggs. As I approached the registration desk, on it there was sign that read "Pressure is on Duty — Ring Bell For Service". I rang the small bell on the counter, and I could hear something coming down a creaking staircase that must have been located behind the open doorway behind the desk. Out of the doorway came a small hairy creature with blue and orange fur. He was about four feet tall and spoke in a deep raspy voice. "So, this is what pressure looks like," I thought to myself. I told him that I had come to say good–bye to him and that I would not be staying in his hotel anymore. He said that he had enjoyed having me as his guest and that he hoped that I had learned something during my stay after all. He said, "I'm not all bad, at times I helped you focus your concentration more strongly. And you played some great golf while under my influence." I nodded in agreement. "By the way," he said, "you still have to pay your bill".

"How much is it?", I asked.

"$102.73," he answered.

I handed him my Visa card, and he ran the card through the manual Visa card processor. I signed the receipt and he gave me a copy. I noticed behind the desk were several rows of mail slots and in one of the slots was a message for Chuck Ruttan. "Does Chuck Ruttan stay here often?" I asked.

"Oh yes, he's one of our best customers," he answered. "Several more of your friends stayed with us also."

I turned and walked to the door and tried to open it, but it was locked. I turned around, and he smiled and pushed a buzzer which opened the door. I ran out the door and up the dark stairway. There was another door at the top of the stairs which I flung open. I was free at last! Outside, I was in the downtown area of a large city. The air was fresh and clean and there were tall buildings all around me.

I waved for a taxi and got into the back seat and away we went. I didn't tell the driver where to take me, but somehow he had a destination in mind, and he drove me there in silence. In a few minutes we were out of the city and we were driving through a redwood forest. The trees were huge. Most had trunks that were wider than the car. We kept following this winding road through the forest until we came to a golf club. The sign on one side of the gate read "Pleasuredale Country Club — For Those Who Play the Game."

The cab driver dropped me off in front of the golf shop and unloaded the clubs from the trunk. I carried my clubs around the side of the building and went into the golf shop. When I walked into the shop, the assistant greeted me and said, "Mr. Aspenson, we've been expecting you. How can we help you?"

"I would like to hit a bucket of balls if I could, " I replied.

"What size bucket would you like," he asked.

"How about a large one?" I answered.

He reached behind the counter and pulled out your typical large yellow bucket of range balls, but the basket only contained five balls. I asked in a surprised tone of voice, "How many balls are in a small bucket?"

"Just one," he answered.

I thanked him and headed out toward the range. The grounds of the club were immaculate, and the course was the most beautiful I had ever seen. It had large fir and redwood trees, peaceful clear blue lakes, and the greenest grass I had ever seen. The people that were playing the course were all smiling and appeared to be enjoying themselves completely.

On my way to the range, I stopped at the putting green and decided to putt for a few minutes first.

On the green the holes all looked huge, about the size of a bucket, probably 12 to 14 inches in diameter. Another man was putting on the practice green, and I asked him if these holes were regulation size.

"Yes," he replied, "four and one–half."

"They sure look a lot larger," I said as I continued to make every putt.

"Many of our members feel the same way," he answered.

I introduced myself. His name was Bob McDuffy. And I went on to explain how I ended up at Pleasuredale. I told him how great it felt to be released from pressure, and he told me that he felt the same way when it happened to him several years ago.

I went on to question him about how to become a member. He said, "All you have to do is demonstrate your ability to play the game."

"What is the course record?" I asked.

"Forty–five," he replied.

"What's par?" I asked.

"Seventy–two," he answered.

"Is it a short course?" I questioned further.

"Sixty–eight hundred yards," he said. He could sense my amazement and went on to say that several of the members shoot in the 40s for 18 holes.

"Come on," Bob said, "I'll show you our range."

We walked down a winding path to the range. "I think you'll enjoy our range," he said.

We came to the teeing area, and there were five or six other people hitting balls. As I looked out on the range, there were no yardage markers, only the images of the other players who were practicing were very visible. As I looked out, I saw a speeding passenger train, a giant frog slowly hopping along, and several different greens were present. All the images were very clear but were only present for a moment.

I pulled the first of my five balls out of the bucket and decided to use my driver. As I took a few practice swings, I could hear the club moving back and forth with the same sound as Darth Vader's laser sword. What a feeling of power! I stepped up to the ball and swung. The ball rocketed off the clubface and became an Indianapolis racing car as it took the banked turn to the right, just as I had pictured the trajectory of my left–handed draw. I smiled and asked Bob, "What's next?"

"Have you ever made a 150–yard putt?" he asked.

"No," I answered as I laughed.

"Give it a try," he suggested.

I pulled the putter out of the bag and put down my second ball. I smoothly stroked the putt and watched the ball as it rolled up and down and left and right over the most undulating green I had ever seen. After rolling what looked to be 150 yards, I saw the ball disappear into a hole which was hardly visible. Again, I felt extremely satisfied.

As I reached for the third ball, I said, "How about a sand shot? Where is the practice bunker?"

"You're standing in it." he said.

Sure enough, even though I hadn't moved, I was now standing in a sand bunker. "Is this about the same texture as the sand on the course?" I asked.

"It is in one of the bunkers. We have sand from all over the world here. Every bunker is different. It adds to the fun and challenge," Bob said.

"How do you know how the ball will react coming out of the different types of sand?"

"By smell," he answered. "You can smell if the sand is damp and heavy or dry and powdery, and adjust accordingly."

I nodded and struck my shot out of the bunker. As it reached the peak of its trajectory, the ball became the Lunar Module and came down gently to the green. A man in a space suit came out of the space craft with a golf ball the size of a basketball under his arm and threw it into the hole. It was incredible!

My fourth shot was a five iron off the grass. I hit it perfectly and as it sailed through the air, I could bend the ball's flight in either direction. It finally came down about 200 yards out. Just as it landed, a green appeared and the ball dropped softly into the hole.

For my fifth and final ball, I asked Bob what to hit.

He asked what club had been giving me problems.

"One iron," I replied. "I've been hitting it off the toe lately."

"Hand me the club," Bob said. As he held onto the shaft, he pulled the toe of the club off. All that was remaining was the sweet spot.

How could I miss, I thought to myself. As I struck the shot, it sailed off perfectly, heading right toward a green that looked like one I had seen during the U.S. Open at Winged Foot. The pin was tucked just two feet over a deep bunker. The ball landed five feet past the pin and spun back into the hole.

Bob and I walked back toward the clubhouse. I was feeling so good. "What city are we in, Bob?" I asked.

"Where would you like to be? There's a Pleasuredale in every city."

We walked toward the parking lot as I prepared to leave. "Could we play tomorrow?"

"Sure," he answered, "Nine o'clock?"

"Sounds great," I replied. "Say, I also know of another guy who would be a great member here at Pleasuredale. His name is Chuck Ruttan. He is still feeling Pressure, but I expect him to be here any day now."

"I'll look forward to meeting him," Bob McDuffy said, as he left.

Just then a taxi pulled up and there was Chuck in the back seat.

I was so excited. "Chuck, get your clubs and I'll pick up a large bucket and meet you on the range. You won't believe it!"

Rid Yourself of Irritations

Two other tools are very helpful in maintaining optimum levels of physical relaxation and mental engagement. They are perceptual flexibility and objectification. The first of these is the awareness that a situation can be viewed in more than one way. You always have the option to interpret the result of a shot or being paired with your least favorite golfing partner or winning or losing so that it is to your advantage. If a tee shot duck hooks into the woods, you can perceive it as an opportunity to create a shot out of demanding and challenging circumstances. This may be the most outstanding shot of your life. If you're paired with the most notorious change–jiggler in existence, you can decide that the noise of the change is money in the bank and is the happiest swing trigger to date. If you win, you can accept that your images were clear, controlled and appropriate, and that you maintained an effective level of physical relaxation and mental engagement. Congratulate yourself. If you lose, you can view it as an opportunity to improve your image clarity and levels of relaxation. For instance, there are many viewers who would agree that even though Calvin Peete won the 1985 TPC tournament, D.A. Weibring won it too. Although he trailed off the lead by three strokes, he played flawless, target–oriented golf. Most important, D.A. saw himself as a winner when all was said and done. "I didn't lose the tournament; Calvin won it," may well have been what he thought about it. Is the glass half empty or half full? You decide. It's your perception, your reality, and your image.

Objectification is a technique for disposing of thoughts and emotions that are not to your advantage. Disappointment is an emotion we are all familiar with. Physically, it can translate into tension or stress. Some people find that disappointment locates in their throat, their head, their stomach, or their chest. When you objectify, you take that vague feeling and turn it into an imaginary object which you dispose of and then replace with another object that you like. These are the four steps:

1. Identify the emotion and locate it in your body.
2. Use all of your senses to turn that emotion into an object. Give it a size, shape, color, texture, temperature, smell, and determine whether or not it makes any noises.
3. Dispose of this object. Mentally image it as you launch it into space, flush it down a toilet, or send it to the center of the earth.
4. Replace the object with something you like. Something that you perceive will contribute to you being relaxed and mentally engaged.

An example of this would be that you have just hit a great shot right in front of the green, and it took a bounce that caused the ball to land in the bunker on the right rather than roll straight for the hole. You review your image and decide that it was 100 percent clear and that you were relaxed enough to respond to the image. So you give your image a ten. Still, the ball is in the bunker. You look to your perceptual flexibility and realize that this is an opportunity to create a great recovery shot. However, you notice that your stomach is tied in knots, and you have a definite feeling of disappointment. You've located and identified the feeling. Now you turn it into an object: It's red, very hot, the size of a loaf of bread, weighs about ten pounds, makes a sizzling sound, smells like a sewer, the texture is very coarse, and it has little spikes all over it. To get rid of it, you put on an asbestos glove (because it's so hot that you don't want to touch it) and hurl it into the water on the next fairway. All the water evaporates because of the object's heat, and it dissolves into the ground. You replace the object with chocolate–almond ice cream because you love the flavor and it will keep you cool and relaxed for the next shot.

The entire process of objectification can happen in ten seconds as you practice it. There is ample opportunity off the course as well as on. Waiting in line, catching all the red lights, an incompetent sales clerk, spilling coffee down your shirt, and finding the puppy chewing up your new shoes are all experiences you have that you can objectify. The purpose of both objectification and perceptual flexibility is to rid yourself of irritations and tensions that build up and prevent you from devoting 100 percent to each shot.

Journal

Keep notes of your practice sessions and of the images you have during a round of golf in a journal. Here are the categories:

1. Imagery practice
2. Relaxation practice
3. Stock images
4. Objectification
5. Perceptual flexibility
6. Pre– and post–round preview
7. Reading
8. Physical practice

The only category that may need explanation at this point is stock images. These are images you have had that really interested and engaged you. Enter them and then you will be able to remember them later on when you're searching for fresh images. Otherwise you run the risk of forgetting several great images you know can work for you.

Your journal entries will also help you develop your story–telling abilities. Writing takes a lot of focused brain power, and the process will help strengthen your experiences and keep them real for you. Your journal is the best support system you can develop for yourself. As you write, you will find images spill out that you had forgotten or were never fully aware of when they first occurred. You can refer back to your entries for ideas and to get an overview of how much progress you have made since you started practicing mental imagery and relaxation.

Goal Setting and Time Management

The skills of goal setting and time management are widely used in the business world. Apply these skills to your golf game as well. When you have clearly defined golfing goals and daily time management, you eliminate a bag–full of woulds, shoulds, coulds, and if only–isms. You also guide yourself away from the *I'll start tomorrow* or *as soon as I can* syndrome. A very effective way to set goals is to start in the future and work your way backwards.

When I work with the touring professionals, I have them start their goal setting at 10 to 20 years in the future. This helps them clarify why they are out on the tour in the first place. It gives them a broad perspective on their career that helps them narrow down to today and why their perfor-mance and attitude today is important. Start with what you want to have achieved in your golf three years from today. You may want to lower your handicap by three strokes, you may want to compete in 12 tournaments, place in the top ten in five of them, win one. If those are your three year goals then what do you have to do in two years to get there in three? Then shift to one year, six months, three months, one week, tomorrow, today. This process gives urgency to to-day. It's easy to say that in three years I need to have my house built, and won't it be fun to start on that tomorrow. Not so much fun if you have no foundation, not to mention the roof by the time three years rolls by. Start today by say-ing that in one week you will have a rough draft of your goals. This first step is the hardest. The rest falls into place once you begin.

When you get down to today, recognize that there are 24 hours to work with. Some of that time you will be sleeping, eating, commuting, working, being with your family, atten-ding to your golf goals. Prioritize these realistically and with flexibility. There will be some months when you have more time for golf than others, and you can plan your time accord-ingly. Remember that the dead of winter in Flint, Michigan, is as good a time as any to mentally rehearse your grip, swing plane, and course management. It may even be the best time, since you won't have to schedule in time on the golf course.

As time passes, reassess your goals regularly. They may change. You may reach them sooner than you projected, or you may find that other priorities present themselves which are more appropriate for you to focus on. When you set goals you construct a triangle. Three years from today is the lower third and point of the triangle. What you do during the next three years funnels in through the top and becomes the substance for generating 100 percent wattage at the bottom of the triangle. Just as each shot has a beginning, middle, and end, so does the process of setting your goals. Your target gives you the information you need to image the trajectory and the way the club needs to be delivered to the ball to send the ball to the target. The end result inspires the reaction and response of the middle and the beginning. Let your three year goals give impact to the way you manage your time today. When you are comfortable that you have aligned yourself with goals that are appropriate to you, you enhance your ability to align yourself on the golf course and to play each shot as it comes. Your triangle of shot efficiency is strengthened.

Goal–setting Chart

A goal-setting chart is shown in figure 61. You can get the most benefit from this chart by doing the following: Use the chart as a visual aid. On a sheet of paper, begin to list your golfing goals for three years from now. Use a pencil because you will probably make several changes. When you have listed these goals, draw a square around them. Now do the same for the two-year goals that help you achieve your three-year goals. When you are finished, draw a box around them and continue with this procedure through one week from now.

There is a list of considerations in the center of the chart. This list includes major elements of your life which will affect the goals you can set for golf. Keep them in mind as you fill out your golfing goals. At first this is going to seem like a lot of work but it will actually relieve you of a lot work once it is completed.

Weekly Time–setting Chart

Figure 62 is a weekly time-setting chart. Photocopy several blanks of the chart. Then make out a list of the time you spend sleeping, eating, etc. Next, determine what blocks of

Figure 61

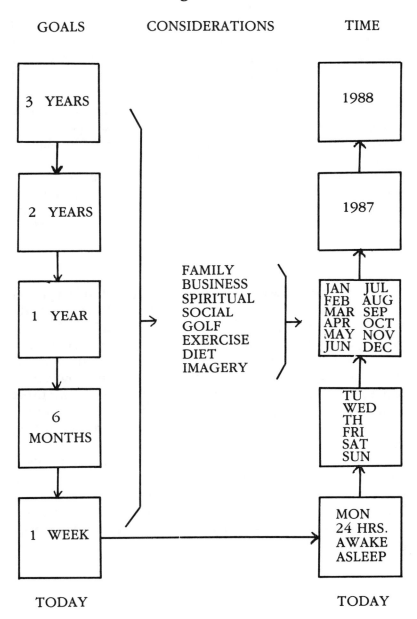

GOALS   CONSIDERATIONS   TIME

3 YEARS

2 YEARS

1 YEAR

FAMILY
BUSINESS
SPIRITUAL
SOCIAL
GOLF
EXERCISE
DIET
IMAGERY

6
MONTHS

1 WEEK

TODAY

1988

1987

JAN   JUL
FEB   AUG
MAR   SEP
APR   OCT
MAY   NOV
JUN   DEC

TU
WED
TH
FRI
SAT
SUN

MON
24 HRS.
AWAKE
ASLEEP

TODAY

For Week Of: _____

Figure 62   WEEKLY TIME MANAGEMENT CHART

INTENTION OF GOAL	TIME ALLOTTED		ACTUAL TIME SPENT							COMMENTS
	DAILY	WEEKLY	M	T	W	TH	F	S	SU	

time you will dedicate to mental imaging and rehearsal during the course of a day and a week. Enter all your time commitments and goals in the left-hand column and mark down the time you allot each one. As the days pass, mark down how much time you actually spend and what kind of quality that time was. Make comments and change accordingly. For instance, if you allotted 30 minutes per day for imaging and averaged 15, you may conclude that 30 minutes is an inappropriate expectation and shorten the period for the next week.

When you first make out your daily time–management chart, you will probably have enough activity to fill a 38–hour day. Obviously, you will need to make some adjustments. A word of caution is that it is very easy for the mental mechanics and imagery practice to fall by the wayside. It has been true for nearly every professional golfer I have worked with. One morning they wake up and realize that they haven't put in the time they had intended for imagery for several days, even months. It was startling for them to realise that time had slipped away even when they had a high degree of intention not to let it slip away. Keep up on your journal entries and there will be less chance of that happening to you. You will constantly be monitoring your involvement. In the field of mental imagery you must be your own best friend. You must fill the double role of teacher and student. You have to keep presenting yourself with activities to keep yourself involved, and you have to make those activities fun and desirable. You need to let the images keep you fresh and interested.

Figure 63 is a monthly time-management chart with categories already filled in. Make several blanks of this and use it to monitor the fluxes that arise due to changing work schedules, vacations, seasonal changes, etc. Notice there are lines dedicated to *Updating Goals* and *Time Management* and *Slob Time*. The slob time is not to be neglected. It is time for you to unplug and do nothing. Some people take the time for extra sleep, some to watch t.v. and eat ice cream, some to sit and do absolutely nothing of importance whatsoever. We all need it to some degree and scheduling it in will assure you that you will get it. A monthly update of your goals (from

Figure 63 MONTHLY TIME MANAGEMENT CHART

For Month of: _____

INTENTION OF GOAL	TIME ALLOTED DAILY	TIME ALLOTED WEEKLY	ACTUAL TIME SPENT DAILY	ACTUAL TIME SPENT WEEKLY	QUALITY OF ACCOMPLISHMENT 100-80	80-60	60-40	40-20	20-0%	COMMENTS
Indoor Imaging										
Relaxation Practice										
Journal Entries										
Physical Exercise Program										
Dietary Monitoring reading, menu preparation										
Physical Mechanics Practice										
Objectification Practice										
Attitude Monitoring										
Supportive Reading										
Competitive Preparation:										
Mental Rehearsal										
Practice Rounds										
Environmental Rapport										
Post Event Review										
Social Commitment:										
Family										
Professional										
Friends										
Updating Goals & Time Management										
Slob Time										
Other:										

three years in the future to the present), and time–management expectations and orientations will keep you abreast of your own growth rate and actual desires.

Make Time for Yourself

One suggestion I have for you to help squeeze 38 hours into 24 is to use the time when you first wake up in the morning or the time right before you go to sleep at night as times to practice relaxation and imagery. Your brain waves are slower at these times than during your waking hours, so you will be able to have clear images and satisfying relaxation sessions. At first, determine which of those times is best for you. It may be easier for you to stick with what you want to do at one time than the other. When you first begin, your mind may wander more than you prefer. Let that happen, notice that you did, and objectively and calmly lead yourself back to the topic you were addressing.

You can double up various tasks to save hours in your day as well. Practice objectification while you drive to work. Verbalize affirmations to yourself anytime, anyplace. Take ten minutes at the office and tell your secretary to take messages and let you be. Use this time to go over deep breathing, autogenics, or imaging your next round of golf. Read other books about imagery during your lunch. Remember to make regular journal entries so that you recognize how much you accomplish during these various bits of time. Most of all, remember to be kind to yourself. Be an objective observer of yourself living your life and yourself playing your golf game. After a month of piano lessons you would not expect yourself to play like Bach. Give yourself the same latitude in your development of images and relaxation skills. Remember that there is no quick fix and that it is a journey, not a destination. There will always be something just around the corner to explore and something else to achieve. Once you knock the three strokes off your game in three years and have played and placed in those tournaments, there will be more strokes to shave off and more tournaments to tackle. Your self–monitoring will become more and more acute, and you will discover new kinds of sensitivities in your grip and the *feel* of the shot. Keep at it and keep having fun at it.

The reading list in Appendix C offers you a start in gleaning information and insight into the history, evolution, and various disciplines that have centered on imagery and mental mechanics. You are not alone. You may be the only golfer on your block who spends a half–hour a day imaging sand shots, but there are and have been many, many others who value spending their time in such endeavors.

Goal setting, objectification, relaxation, pre– and post–round preparation, and the other topics I have presented in this book are all skills which are components of confidence. Regular rehearsal and practice of these skills will enhance your ability to achieve your maximum performance potential. Adding these skills to your physical skills in golf will make your game more balanced and fun. One skill will foster another and you will have many to draw upon as you play the game with increasingly more enjoyment.

Figure 64 is a graph you can use to plot your confidence components. Draw a line from zero to the percentage that you feel you have accomplished in each category. Start with where you are today, make frequent updates, and keep them to compare with the plot you have in a year. You will appreciate the differences.

This is the same graph the pros have used to support the use of mental imagery in practice and competition. When each professional started the physical mechanics category was at 100 percent and physical exercise was something in excess of 65 percent. All the other categories, however, averaged less than 50 percent. As they have practiced and upgraded these other categories, they have significantly dropped their scores. In less than a year of working with S.E.A. the men have dropped from .07 to 1.7 strokes and the women have dropped up to 3 strokes. At the professional level, these improvements are significant.

Through daily practice of the various components of confidence, you will strengthen the walls of your processing triangle and add trust to your intuitive processes. The final epic of your shot processing will be very strong — totally resistant to intrusive thoughts.

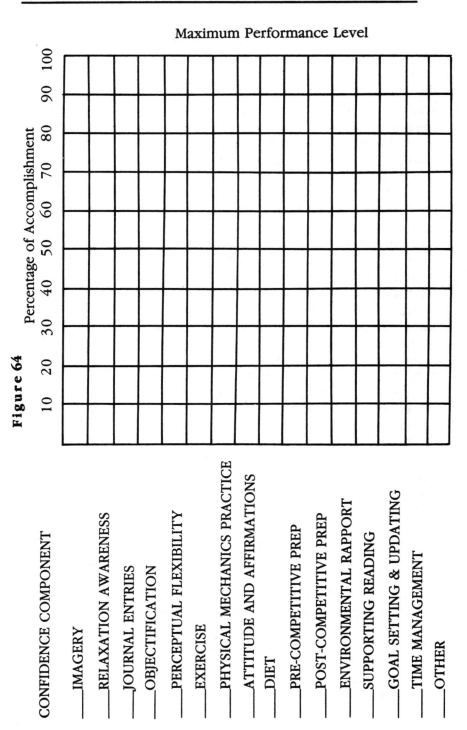

Figure 64

Here is a general guide list for the next few years:

1. Read other books to increase your knowledge and awareness of imagery.
2. Develop and maintain systems for self–monitoring: Journal, time–management, etc.
3. Continually foster and improve your perceptual flexibility. Keep finding and opening new doors.
4. Continually update goals and time management.
5. Breathe with intent.
6. Satisfy, maintain and upgrade physical strength, flexibility, and responsibility. Get the proper exercise and follow the proper diet.
7. Use imagery to keep yourself healthy and to reduce the length of illnesses and recovery periods.
8. Explore sleep control and dream awareness. (See *Creative Dreaming* by Patricia Garfield.)
9. Learn about quantum mechanics and the holographic brain model theory. (See the supportive reading list.)
10. Continue to remember your zip code, brush your teeth, get your beauty sleep, have a nice day, and get on with being an active, effective imager every day.

Potential is a loaded word. No person will actually reach and sustain their fullest potential. This is not only okay; it is desirable. It is the quest that makes the game worth playing — life worth living.

One last thing: sometimes you'll be tempted to say to yourself "Well, these imaging skills are important, but this tournament is more important. I'll use imaging sometime when it is not as important." Don't do it that way. Use the skills you have learned in this book all of the time, starting right now. If it is important to win a tournament or a round or even just play one hole well, then it is important to use your new skills. They will improve your game all of the time. Play the game and be the most active reactor on your block, and then you will always remember:

After the swing there shall be golf.

Appendix A

Glossary

This short glossary is concept–oriented. I have taken some liberties with the definitions of some of the terms. However, these definitions will give you a feeling for how people who study the mental side of sports use these terms.

Afferent: The act of carrying nerve impulses from the body to the nerve center.

Brain: A mass of nerve tissue inside the cranium that transmits and receives impulses.

Concept: The abstract form of an idea or notion.

Confidence: A state of firm belief, trust, and reliance in yourself and your abilities.

Efferent: The act of carrying nerve impulses from the nerve center into the body.

Eu-: A prefix meaning good or well being.

Eustress: Eustress is the healthy level of stress which every person has. The specific level varies from individual to individual, but it is a shared phenomenon among all people.

Frequency following response: The process of slowing down and harmonizing brain waves. It specifically describes the synchronization and harmonization of brainwaves with the sound waves produced by the MS III Image Generator.

Habit: An acquired pattern of action.

Holography: A method of recording three–dimensional information on a two–dimensional plate from which an image can be reconstructed.

Human potential: The capabilities and possibilities which have yet to come into being. The result of exploration into inner space.

Hypnogogic: The period of time just before you fall to sleep. Also known as pre–sleep.

Hypnopompic: The period of time just before you become consciously awake after sleeping.

Imagery: The internal, non–verbal processing of sensory perceptions which may or may not be externally stimulated. Includes processing of all sensory modalities: visual, kinesthetic, auditory, olfactory, and taste.

Intuition: Direct knowledge of something without conscious reasoning.

Luck: The seemingly chance happening of events which affect you. A convenient way not to take responsibility.

Mind: The seat of consciousness; that which thinks, perceives, feels, calculates, reasons. The director of all physical activity including response to the physical world.

Muscle memory: A mythical state in which muscles remember things instead of the brain. As valid as moustache memory, clothing memory, hair memory, and fingernail memory. In other words, if your muscles are capable of remembering how to swing the club, then your shirt should be able to remember also.

Objectification: A process whereby an emotional state is identified, internally located, turned into an object (through imagery), discarded, and replaced by another object perceived to be more beneficial.

Pacing: An internal tempo characteristically unique to each individual.

Perception: Insight, intuition, knowledge, or understanding which is mentally grasped through sensory awareness. It is real to the perceiver.

Perceptual flexibility: The ability to understand that there is more than one way to interpret an event or situation.

Play: To have fun and participate, perform and be engaged in an activity.

Pressure: A feeling of stress, urgency, or weight being forced into your emotional state.

Psychophysics: The science dealing with the physiological interaction within your body/mind unit.

Quantum physics: The science of dealing with discreet sub–atomic matter as it relates to energy exchange.

Synesthesia: The perception of a sense other than the one being stimulated; cross sensing.

Trust: To have confidence, faith, and commitment in your own reliability.

Will power: Strength of mind, determination, self–control.

Appendix B

Strenghening and Stretching Exercises For a Better Golf Game

By Hilloah Rohr, M.S. Exercise Physiology
© 1984 Body Tuning
Used with the permission of the author

The Warm Up

Warming up properly can be regarded as an essential prelude to ensuring the readiness of the body for physical activity. Memorize the following sequence of exercises and carefully proceed through them before each time you play. Each exercise is to be performed in a relaxed, rhythmic manner. Go smoothly from one exercise directly to the next, breathe long and deep, and keep the movement slow so you can experience your full range of motion. Enjoy!

Exercise	Repetitions	Description
1. Head Directions	2-4 ea. direction	Front/back, side/side, ear to shoulder.
2. Shoulder Rolls	4 back, 4 forward	Large, slow circles.
3. Arm Swings	10-15	Swing arms across chest, open wide to sides.

1

2

3

4. Arm
   Circles
10-15
Cross arms front, open over head and wide to sides.

5. Side
   Swings
10-15
Keep hips stationary, swing arms side to side.

6. Side Bend
2-4 ea. side
Straight to side, support stretch with hand on leg.

7. Hamstring
   Stretch
2-4 ea. side
Leg elevated comfortably, hips square, foot straight.

8. Shoulder
   Stretch
2 ea.
direction
Keeping the rest of the body aligned, interlace hands and stretch shoulders back, then reverse and cross hands, interlace and pull forward.

4

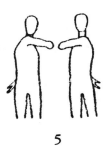

5

6

7

8

Strengthening Exercises

The following exercises were specially chosen to specifically strengthen the muscles involved in the golf game. Be sure to keep the breath full during the exercises, exhaling on the exertion phase. Do not hold the breath!

Each exercise should be done with good technique, isolating the desired muscle group. The motion should be explosive, but smooth on the resistance phase, and slow on the lowering phase. A full range of motion should be applied as much as possible, always keeping the correct form.

A progression of repetitions is shown. Start at the lower end and work up. Sets (repeat groups of repetitions) may be practiced to increase benefits when a harder workout is desired and the muscles are physically ready.

These strengthening exercises should be practiced a minimum of 3 times per week.

1. Abdominal Crunches — 10-40 reps — Easy: arms reaching towards knees, med: arms crossed on shoulders, hard: finger tips on head. Keep chin tucked in, lift and hold, lower slowly.

2. Twisting Crunches — 10-40 reps — Knees up, opposite elbow to knee, hands behind head, lift and hold, lower slowly.

3. Leg Switches — 10-20 — Low back stays flat on ground. Start with legs up high, lower angle towards floor, switching knees to chest until back almost arches, keep pushing low back to floor.

1   2   3

4. Erect Pelvic Tilt and Lowering	6-10	Press low back to wall, pull pelvis from wall - slowly bend knees and lower and raise body, keeping back to wall and pelvis away.
5. Back Leg Raise	8-16 complete	Keeping both hips on the ground, lift straight leg from the hip, hold and lower - alternate legs.
6. Arm and Leg Raise	8-16 complete	Lift opposite arm and leg, head and chest, hold and lower - alternate legs.
7. Side Bends	8-16 complete	Standing, arms over head holding cord taught, bend smoothly straight to side, return, repeat.
8. Sitting Twists	8-16 complete	Sitting with legs straddling bench - golf club or bar behind neck - gently twist side to side.
9. Bridges	10-30	On back, knees bent, feet close to hips - raise hips high as is comfortable, lower, repeat.

5

6

4

7

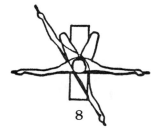

8

9

10. Bent Rows and Shrugs — 10-15 ea. — Bent over, knees slightly bent, cord wrapped under feet, pull cord to armpits, lower, repeat. Shrugs: arms straight, squeeze shoulder blades together towards mid back, release.

11. Shoulder Press — 10-15 — Cord extends from under feet and is taught at shoulder level - keep hips tucked under, back straight - extend cord overhead, bring down behind head, extend, lower back to front, repeat.

12. Tricep Extensions — 10-15 — Lean over, knees slightly bent, arms bent, elbows high - extend cord back using lower arms only and return, keeping elbows high.

13. Wrist Extension — 8-10 — Sit with wrists resting on knees, hands palm down, holding a golf club or use a taught cord, extending away from body - smoothly extend wrist back - return.

10

11

12

13

| 14. Wrist Twists | 10-25 | Sit with wrists resting on knees, hold a bar or weight in each hand - smoothly twist in and out. |
| 15. Hand Squeezes | 10-25 | Hold a compressible object, such as a ball or grip strengthener in each hand - squeeze rhythmically until the muscles are fatigued. |

14   15

Deep Relaxing Stretches

Best results come when these stretches are done when the body is already warmed up. After golf and before bed are good times. These deep relaxing stretches can help reduce the next day stiffness and soreness.

The key to successful stretching is to:
1) <u>avoid overstretching</u> - stretch only to where you feel a comfortable pull
2) <u>relax into the stretch</u> — release the stretch and go back into it if you find yourself tightening up - relax mentally also
3) <u>breathe long and deep</u> while stretching
4) <u>hold the position</u> (no bouncing) for a minimum of 30 seconds, with ideal being 1-3 minutes or until the muscle feels released

Lastly, don't worry about how far you can stretch. The important element is that you feel an easy, even stretch in the desired area.

Specific exercises from this group should be chosen to stretch any areas which have been under stress and strain, as well as areas that are chronically tight. They can be done daily or on occasion, as time permits.

1. Feet Together

Keeping hips forward, relax upper body forward towards feet. *Easier: sit with back to wall.

2. Front Stretch

Keeping hips forward, relax upper body forward, knees straight, ankles together. *Easier: bend one leg.

3. Back Slant

Release to front stretch - lean back on arms and relax jaw, neck, head and shoulders.

4. Knees to Chest

First bring single knees to chest, holding knees from behind leg, then bring both knees to chest, hold and release.

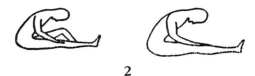

1

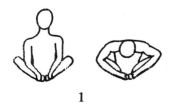

2

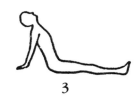

3

4

5. Chair Stretch

Sitting in chair, lower upper body down to where the thighs are supporting the upper body, hold and breathe, roll up starting at base of spine. *A pillow may be placed on lap for less stretch.

6. Wall Arch

Standing 5" away from a wall, place hands on wall, lean shoulders into wall, keeping knees straight, roll down through hips, arching back gently backwards - roll back up in reverse order - align hips and push from wall.

5

6

Appendix C

Bibliography

Abravannel, Dr., *Body Type Program, For Health, Fitness and Nutrition,* 1985, Bantam

Armour, Tommy, *How to Play Your Best Golf All of the Time,* 1985, Ailsa

Bandler, Richard, *Magic in Action,* 1984, META

Bandler, Richard, *Using Your Brain for a Change,* 1985, Real People Press

Bandler, Richard and Grinder, John, *Reframing,* 1982, Real People Press

Bandler, Richard and Grinder, John, *Trance-Formations,* 1982, Real People Press

Bandler, Richard and Grinder, John, *The Structure of Magic II,* 1976, Real People Press

Boomer, Percy, *On Learning Golf,* 1946, Knopf

Brown, Barbara B., *Supermind: The Ultimate Energy,* 1980, Harper and Row

Cambell, Joseph, *The Way of the Animal Powers,* 1983, Van der Marck

Cleveland, Bernard, *Master Teaching Techniques,* 1986, Connecting Link Press

Cousins, Norman, *Anatomy of an Illness as Perceived by the Patient: Reflections of Healing & Regeneration,* 1979, Norton

Edwards, Betty, *Drawing on the Right Side of the Brain,* 1979, J. P. Tarcher

Gallwey, Timothy, *The Inner Game of Golf,* 1981, Random House

Gallwey, Timothy, *The Inner Game of Tennis,* 1979, Bantam

Garfield, Charles A. and Bennent, Hal Z., *Peak Performance: Mental Training Techniques of the World's Greatest Athletes,* 1984, J. P. Tarcher

Garfield, Patricia, *Creative Dreaming,* 1976, Ballantine

Gawain, Shakti, *Creative Visualization,* 1979, Bantam

Gawain, Shakti, *Living in the Light,* 1986, Whatever Publishing

Hampden-Turner, Charles, *Maps of the Mind,* 1982, MacMillan

Illerbrun, *Benji's Daddy Was a Golfer,* 1985, Oolichan Books

James, Jennifer, Ph.D., *Success is the Quality of Your Journey,* 1986, Newmarket Press

Korn, Errol R. and Johnson, Karen, *Visualization: The Uses of Imagery in the Health Professions,* 1983, Dow Jones-Irwin

Leonard, George, *Ultimate Athlete,* 1975, Viking

Maltz, Maxwell, *Psycho-Cybernetics,* 1968, Wilshire

Masters, Robert and Houston, Jean, *Mind Games,* 1973, Dell

Murphy, Michael, *Golf in the Kingdom,* 1973, Dell

Murphy, Michael, *The Psychic Side of Sports,* 1979, Addison-Wesley

Ristad, Eloise, *A Soprano on Her Head: Right-Side-Up Reflections on Life — & Other Performances,* 1982, Real People

Robbins, Anthony, *Unlimited Power,* 1986, Simon and Schuster

Samuels, Mike and Samuels, Nancy, *Seeing with the Mind's Eye,* 1975, Random House

Seyer, John and Connlly, Christopher, *Sporting Body, Sporting Mind: An Athlete's Guide to Mental Training,* 1984, Cambridge University Press

Toben, Bob and Wolf, Fred A., *Space, Time & Beyond,* 1982, Dutton

Vitale, Barbara Meister, *Unicorns Are Real,* 1982, Jalmar Press

Wilber, Ken, *The Holographic Paradigm and Other Paradoxes: Exploring the Leading Edge of Science,* 1982, Shambhala Publications

Wolf, Fred A., *Taking the Quantum Leap: The New Physics for Nonscientists,* 1979, Harper and Row

Zakau, Gary, *The Dancing Wu Li Masters: An Overview of the New Physics,* 1980, Bantam